# The Managing Diversity
# Survival Guide

Lee Gardenswartz and Anita Rowe are partners in the management consulting firm of Gardenswartz & Rowe of Los Angeles, California. For more than 13 years, Gardenswartz & Rowe has specialized in the "human side of management" for a variety of regional and national clients, helping them manage change, handle stress, build productive and cohesive work teams, create intercultural understanding, and increase personal and professional effectiveness.

Lee Gardenswartz is a native of Denver and a graduate of the University of Colorado at Boulder. After working as a secondary teacher and staff development facilitator in the Los Angeles Unified School District for a number of years, she returned to academia and earned her Doctorate in human behavior from the United States International University in 1981. She wrote her dissertation on organizational stress and what a company can do to minimize its negative effects.

Anita Rowe is a native of Los Angeles and a graduate of UCLA. She also worked as a secondary teacher and staff development facilitator in the Los Angeles Unified School District for a number of years and then returned to academia to earn her Doctorate in human behavior from the United States International University in 1981.

Together they have coauthored a series of articles and three books: *Beyond Sanity and Survival*, a stress management workbook; *What It Takes* (Doubleday, 1987), a new model for leadership and achievement; and the best-selling *Managing Diversity* (Irwin Professional Publishing). They write a regular column on diversity for *Managing Diversity* Newsletter, and they are presently at work on a training package for Irwin Professional Publishing entitled *The Diversity Tool Kit*.

Among Gardenswartz & Rowe's clients are GTE, State Farm Insurance Co., TRW, Childrens Hospital of Los Angeles, DWP, The Los Angeles Times, UCLA, Motherhood Maternity, MCA, and Prudential Insurance Co. Anita and Lee have lectured widely, giving keynote speeches, facilitating team-building retreats, and teaching seminars across the country. They have made guest appearances on such programs as "Mid-Morning L.A.," "CNN's News Night," "Sun Up San Diego," "AM Northwest," and the Michael Jackson show.

To communicate with the authors or to gain additional information about their programs and services, contact:

Gardenswartz & Rowe
12658 W. Washington Blvd.
Suite 105
Los Angeles, CA 90066
(310) 823-2466

# The Managing Diversity Survival Guide
## A Complete Collection of Checklists, Activities, and Tips

Lee Gardenswartz

Anita Rowe

Boston, Massachusetts   Burr Ridge, Illinois   Dubuque, Iowa
Madison, Wisconsin   New York, New York   San Francisco, California   St. Louis, Missouri

## McGraw-Hill

*A Division of The **McGraw·Hill** Companies*

*Printed in the United States of America*
6 7 8 9 0 MAL/MAL 0 9 8 7 6 5 4 3

# Preface

*The Managing Diversity Survival Guide: A Complete Collection of Checklists, Activities, and Tips* is a response to the many requests from readers who wish to duplicate materials from *Managing Diversity: A Complete Desk Reference and Planning Guide*. Their calls indicate a desire to use the activities, checklists, charts, and worksheets in diversity-related seminars and workshops. In response, we have provided more than just the requested training materials in reproducible format. Our goal is to provide the content "infrastructure" a trainer would need for most diversity training sessions. To that end, we have also included overhead transparency masters and sample agendas.

Because diversity training differs from other types of training, being more challenging and complex in many ways, it requires additional knowledge and skills on the part of the trainer. To help you in that area, we have provided a self-analysis tool to assess your diversity training strengths and weaknesses, with an implied prescription for improvement. You will also find a discussion of the very real issues that confront anyone who presents diversity seminars in today's organizations, as well as tips that will set you up for success. This section gives you answers to the most frequently asked questions regarding diversity, hints for dealing with resistance, and ways to structure your training agendas for best results. All of the material is designed to minimize trainer stress and participant resistance while maximizing receptivity, openness, and learning.

Lee Gardenswartz
Anita Rowe

# Contents

## SECTION III    TRANSPARENCY MASTERS                                               195

# Section I

# Introduction

"Oh, for the good old days!" is a commonly heard refrain in most organizations. But times have changed, and longing for yesteryear is not a fruitful strategy for meeting the challenges of our era. Part of this changing reality lies in the composition of the population. Demographic shifts are radically altering the makeup of the work force, bringing more women, people of color, and immigrants to the job. Other differences, such as age, sexual orientation, physical ability, education, and values, are also playing an increasingly important role in the workplace, affecting communication, commitment, and ultimately productivity. As a result, visionary and pragmatic organizations realize that developing a climate where differences are truly valued is more than just a good idea—it is a business imperative. Most organizations also recognize that training aimed at increasing the awareness, knowledge, and skills of all employees is an important element in creating an inclusive work environment. From the shop floor to the executive suite, in the field office and in the boardroom, managerial and nonmanagerial staff need help in developing the attitudes, approaches, and techniques they need to function effectively with today's increasingly diverse workforce. This book is designed to give you that help.

# How to Use This Book

The following pages provide resources for those charged with planning and conducting diversity-related training. Over 80 training tools, in the forms of questionnaires, charts, diagrams, and worksheets are presented in reproducible format, ready for use in a training seminar. Each tool is accompanied by suggestions for its use as a training activity. These suggestions state the objectives, intended audience, processing steps, and questions for discussion, as well as caveats and considerations where appropriate.

In addition, masters for overhead transparencies that contain the major concepts are included in Section III. These are intended as lecturette content for the human resources professional and are keyed to relevant pages in *Managing Diversity,* from which the trainer can get additional information about the specific topic. Since various facilitators may use the tools and activities differently, the directions for the participants and the choice of discussion questions are left to the discretion of the trainer. Once you decide how you want the group to proceed with the activity and what questions you want your trainees to use in their discussion groups, you may supplement the prepared transparencies with your own overheads.

You will combine a variety of activities and use different tools for your custom-designed diversity training sessions. To help you tailor your sessions, we include at the end of Section I a few sample agendas showing how to combine various tools and activities in different formats.

# Considerations before You Begin

Before you embark on diversity training, consider the following six questions. Clarifying the purpose of the proposed training and testing the organization's commitment are important initial steps.

1.  **Are there clear symptoms of things gone wrong that have their origins in the diverse mix of your staff? If so, what are they?**   In other words, what's going on that leads you to believe diversity training is needed? Part of the answer can be determined by looking at the *Symptoms* checklist that follows. Cliques, conflicts, complaints, or miscommunication may indicate that some kind of training is needed. Are there people from different backgrounds or cultures who barely communicate? Do you notice subgroups or power struggles drawn along ethnic lines? Can you point to conflicts that seem rooted in the irritation felt when other people don't do things "our" way? Have gender or ethnic slurs or jokes occurred? Do some groups encounter obstacles to promotion? Any of these realities can suggest the need for training. In addition, if turnover is high and exit interviews indicate that good, talented people are leaving because they can't adjust to working with people different from themselves or don't feel fully included in the organization, diversity training is a wise investment.

# Ten Symptoms That May Indicate a Need for Diversity Training

_____   1.   Complaints about insensitive comments made or jokes told in the work unit regarding age, gender, ethnicity, sexual orientation, or physical ability.

_____   2.   Inability to retain members of diverse groups.

_____   3.   Open conflict between groups or between people from different groups.

_____   4.   Lack of diversity throughout _all_ levels of the organization.

_____   5.   Cultural faux pas committed out of ignorance rather than malice.

_____   6.   Diversity-related blocks in communication that impede work flow.

_____   7.   Misinterpreting or not understanding directions, leading to mistakes, repeating tasks, and low productivity.

_____   8.   EEOC suits.

_____   9.   Feeling of isolation from the work group.

_____   10.  Perception that one's strengths and background are not valued for the unique contribution they can make.

## Suggestions for Using Ten Symptoms That May Indicate a Need for Diversity Training

**Objectives:**
- Identify diversity-related problems within the organization.
- Determine if there is a need for diversity training.

**Intended Audience:**
- Managers, supervisors, and employees at all levels who can share their perceptions about the organization.
- Members of project teams such as diversity task forces charged with planning diversity training.
- Training professionals involved in planning and delivering diversity training.

**Processing the Activity:**
- Individuals respond to the checklist, checking off any symptoms they observe in the organization.
- Checklists are then collected and tabulated, and the results are used by the requesting individual or group.
- Alternatively, participants share their responses in a group discussion and determine the most commonly perceived symptoms.

**Questions for Discussion:**
- What are the most commonly perceived symptoms?
- What is the impact of these symptoms on productivity, morale, and teamwork?
- Which symptoms relate to issues and problems that training can help resolve? Which deal with organizational systems and policies?

**Caveats and Considerations:**
- The *Symptoms* checklist is not an exhaustive listing. Respondents may wish to add other symptoms based on their own experiences in the organization.
- Like any needs assessment instrument, this tool will lead participants to bring up problems. Once elicited, concerns need to be dealt with, not shelved. Make sure that the data generated are used in planning any interventions indicated and that respondents are told what will be done.

2.  **Is the training relevant?**   The issue of *relevance* is also critical. Training should apply to participants' everyday realities and make them better able to deal with the thorny issues they confront in their jobs. Even as an internal human resources professional, you can play the role of external consultant and ask some clarifying questions of those requesting the training. The following questions may help:

    - What are your goals and objectives?
    - What's going on that indicates you need this training?
    - How do you define the problem?
    - How would other people on the staff define the problem?
    - What specific changes or results do you want to see as a consequence of this training?
    - What outcomes must you see to know that the investment has been worth the organization's time, energy, and money?
    - What resources are you willing to commit to accomplish your goals and objectives?
    - Who else needs to be interviewed before this training takes place?

    Collecting this kind of information should enable you to design on-target training.

    A postscript here regarding relevance in this era of TQM (total quality management) and collaboration: Diversity training is particularly effective when incorporated into team building. Though it is often a more circuitous route to racial and ethnic understanding, it can have far-reaching effects on work group understanding and effectiveness, no matter how much individuals differ in culture or lifestyle. When used as an aid to team functioning, diversity training engenders more commitment.

3.  **Is there real support for the training?**   Will the time and money allocated to the training effort demonstrate that it is an important priority? Token support is demoralizing. When training is not considered valuable enough for top management to attend—or for employees to be released from their regular duties to participate—the number of participants dwindles, skepticism grows, and training in general becomes a tolerated nuisance.

    All training must have management support, but such support is even more critical for diversity training. The diversity issue brings out built-in fears and resistance, sometimes rational but frequently irrational. When there is demonstrated support at the top, the resistance tends to diminish over time, and real progress in the form of increased cohesion and enthusiasm for work can be seen.

4.  **Does the training have clearly defined purposes?**   Has the groundwork been laid so that all participants know why they are there? When planning these sessions, ask yourself what trainees will be able to do after the session that they could not do before. State objectives specifically and in behavioral terms so results can be measured. Whatever your purpose for the training, it needs to be clearly defined, presented for all to see, and measurable. It also needs to be publicized ahead of time so participants walk in with a clear idea of the purpose and get no surprises once the session starts.

5.  **Are sessions structured so that trainees actively participate?**   People internalize learning more effectively when they *hear, see,* and *do.* A combination

of self-assessment, lecture, role play, and discussion sustains participants' interest and involvement. Most important, training sessions must apply to real-life work situations, problems, and issues.

Further, the most effective diversity training emphasizes common ground. For example, I can see that you look different from me. But when I learn, through participating in training activities, that we both value our families, have hopes and dreams for our children, and struggle to live purposeful, meaningful lives, our cultural differences are merely window dressing rather than a major chasm. This awareness doesn't occur in the absence of interactive learning.

6. **Is there a commitment to follow-up, by both participants and management, that goes beyond lip service?** In some organizations, diversity training begins and ends with personal awareness regarding attitudes, prejudices, and fears. This is a necessary first step, but it is not sufficient if you want to change the culture. In other organizations, training goes beyond awareness to knowledge about what culture really is and then offers specific information about certain cultures and the range of differences in norms. The most thorough training combines awareness and knowledge with skill development. For example, how does one handle conflicts, run meetings, and give feedback to diverse staff? One way to encourage the use and reinforcement of these skills is to make the new behaviors part of the performance appraisal. Building action plans and follow-up steps is critical for the training to have any impact. Accountability and implementation are best ensured when bosses and trainees work hand in hand to apply newly learned strategies and skills on the job.

Answering the above six questions can help you determine what, if any, kind of training should be undertaken. More important, with an appropriate long-range attitude, a realistic set of objectives, and training that is tailored to your organization, the results can more than justify the investment.

# Answering the Questions That Can Sabotage Diversity Training Efforts

Whether you are selling diversity training to executive management or to the participants in your sessions, you need to answer both the stated and unstated questions up front. If not dealt with, these questions can plant the seeds of resistance and undermine your results. Below are answers to some of the questions we most frequently hear.

1. **Why are we doing this?** Explaining the demographic changes in the work force (OH 1–1), followed by additional information about the population shifts in your region and in your organization specifically, is a start. You may follow with a discussion of changes that participants have seen and are presently dealing with, in both the organization and the customer base.

2. **What has diversity got to do with us?** This question may require an explanation of the business imperative that diversity presents, showing that the organization's long term survival is at stake (OH 1–2) as well as pointing out the pragmatic benefits to the individual. For example, learning how to communi-

cate across language barriers may be especially helpful to supervisors of employees who speak limited English or to staff with high customer contact who deal with a multicultural customer base. Developing strategies for resolving conflicts may be useful to managers with fractionalized teams. Or developing coaching skills may give managers the tools they need to mentor and nurture diverse staff members.

3. **What is diversity?**   Even in sophisticated organizations, a definition of terms may be in order. It is important to have a common frame of reference and a clear definition to minimize confusion. A short lecturette, followed by a discussion of the primary and secondary dimensions of diversity from Loden and Rosener (OH 1–3), may help attendees understand that we are all part of the diversity puzzle and that diversity goes beyond dealing with race and gender. Frequently this broad definition helps clarify the business imperative for resistant participants. The discussion also gives participants a chance to share perceptions about how these dimensions affect them and their staffs.

4. **What is the difference between managing diversity and affirmative action?**   Often participants make comments that indicate confusion about the difference between affirmative action and managing diversity. "Isn't this just affirmative action with a new coat of paint?" they ask. An explanation of the key differences—clarifying the various motivations, strategies, and objectives of these initiatives—may be helpful at this point (OH 1–4). Especially helpful may be distinguishing among legal, moral, and pragmatic organizational motivations.

5. **Does this mean we have to lower our standards?**   Quality-versus-diversity perceptions are the root of this question. Resistance may arise among participants who think the emphasis on diversity is antithetical to quality. Dealing with this question may call for a discussion of different ways to view the relationship between quality and diversity (OH 1–5). But the important point is that quality and diversity are not mutually exclusive; they can and do occur in the same employee.

# Caveats in Conducting Diversity Training

A former colleague, Dr. Marc Robert, used to warn us, "Don't open up a can of worms if you don't have the recipe for worm soufflé." Diversity training can bring some wormy issues to the surface, and few societies or organizations have created effective recipes to make them palatable. However, forewarned is forearmed. Anticipating potential difficulties in your training sessions can help you prepare to deal with them as they arise and perhaps even avoid some of them.

1. **Heightened emotionality and tension.**   Diversity deals with many sensitive issues about which people are apt to have strong feelings and opinions. Since we were raised in a society that tells us it is wrong to be prejudiced, just talking about these topics breaks social taboos and hence produces tension. Most of us find it difficult to admit to our own biases and stereotypic assumptions. As a result, anger, confusion, frustration, and dismay are common. Building an accepting, safe training environment in which people feel comfortable voicing these feelings is essential.

2. **Danger of polarization.**   An age-old dictum warns us not to talk about reli-

gion and politics at parties for fear that a polarizing argument will ensue. The same dictum could be reframed around issues of race, ethnicity, and sexual orientation. In diversity training sessions, there is a danger that participants will fall into an either/or trap about topics that bring out strong emotional reactions, such as those regarding language (Should we have English-only rules?)(Should gays be allowed in the military?). These polarizing discussions create arguments and no-win situations that split a group into warring camps.

It is critical to help the group see other options and develop ways to look at such situations in a new light. It is also important to steer the discussion to situations, practices, and policies over which participants have some control and away from opinions and dead-end values arguments.

3. **People with personal axes to grind.**   Trainees bring their own baggage into diversity sessions. In some cases, a backlog of unresolved issues causes a participant to come into the session with a personal agenda that disrupts other trainees' learning. Focusing on examples such as one poorly handled organizational problem or one particular incident of discrimination skews the discussion, may polarize the group, and divert the training from its main points. Strong facilitation skills are required to keep the group on track.

4. **People getting boxed into corners.**   Because individuals hold strong opinions about many diversity issues, they may box one another into corners with personal attacks and labels. It is important to create a climate in which everyone is treated with respect and no one loses dignity. You can ensure such a climate by establishing ground rules at the beginning and then enforcing them.

5. **Wide range of reactions.**   In your sessions, expect a range of reactions and attitudes from denial and hostility to acceptance and relief that the training is finally taking place. Some trainees will deny that any problems exist—("We all get along here" or "I'm not prejudiced; I treat everyone the same."). Others may resent having to attend the sesions ("Why are we spending money on this when I just took a 5 percent pay cut?") Some may be upset about the changing demographics ("When in Rome, do as the Romans do. Why do I have to learn about them?"). Still others may welcome the training ("It's about time we talked about these issues."). Creating a climate in which these different views can be both expressed and addressed needs to be part of the agenda.

6. **White Male Bashing.**   Because white males have been the dominant group in American society and business, it is tempting to make them the target of blame. It is important to help trainees see that all of us are products of socialization and cultural programming and that no one group has the corner on the market when it comes to discrimination and prejudice. Helping participants see beyond labels and assumptions to the complexity of each human being is essential. It is also helpful to allow white male participants to air the difficulties and dilemmas they face in adapting today's diverse and rapidly changing world.

7. **Timing.**   While timing is not everything in life, it is an important consideration in diversity training. Holding sessions while your company is downsizing or negotiating a contract with the union is apt to be counterproductive. There may never be a  perfect time, but some periods are clearly better than others.

8. **Danger of lip service.**   Conducting diversity training because the business magazines tout it as the latest fad or because someone in HR feels it is important is a setup for disappointment. Training is most effective when it is part of a larger plan for managing diversity, and that plan needs tie into your organiza-

tion's strategic objectives. Having the real support of executive management means you will be able to remove systems obstacles and make policy changes to create a more inclusive organization. If trainees do not perceive this genuine commitment, they are apt to discount the value of the training no matter how well it is done.

What does your analysis tell you about your planning? What do you need to do to shore up your preparations to ensure effective training? The *Diversity Training Planning Checklist* can help you plan your training program and sessions. Using this checklist as a planning guide and again as a post-session evaluation tool can help you continually improve your training. You may find additional assistance in *Managing Diversity,* Chapter 5, ''Making Meetings Work in a Culturally Diverse Environment.''

# Diversity Training Planning Checklist

Directions: Check those conditions and actions to which you have attended in your planning.

### Laying the Foundation in the Organization

_____ Diversity is seen and understood as a business imperative.

_____ There is top-level understanding about how diversity connects to the organization's strategic objective.

_____ There is commitment from the executive level to making the necessary systems and policy changes.

_____ Top-level executives have committed to participating in diversity training.

_____ Training is one part of a larger diversity effort throughout the organization.

### Preplanning

_____ Publicity for the training emphasizes the benefits for all attendees.

_____ Training is scheduled at the least disruptive times possible and, when feasible, options regarding which session to attend are offered.

_____ Training sites are conducive to learning.

_____ Some form of needs assessment (interviews, focus groups, questionnaire) has been conducted so that trainees' needs are clear.

_____ Necessary equipment and sufficient materials are ready and available.

_____ Participants are scheduled to attend in diverse groups.

_____ Refreshments have been arranged.

### The Training Session Agenda

_____ The purpose and objectives of the session are clearly communicated to participants at the beginning.

_____ The objectives of the training are relevant to participants' needs and issues.

_____ The objectives and activities planned realistically match the time allotted.

_____ A quick, purposeful, and focusing warmup is planned for the beginning of the session.

_____ There is a variety of activities and groupings.

_____ The agenda is structured so that participation is elicited from all attendees.

_____ Ample time is allotted for participants to process information and share reactions.

_____ Application to real on-the-job situations is emphasized.

_____ Pairs and small groups are used to increase comfort, safety, and collegiality.

_____ Processes are structured to allow opportunity for sharing and airing different views.

### Evaluation and Closure

_____ There is an opportunity for participants to share their insights, learnings, and "so-whats."

_____ Feedback about the session is solicited from participants.

_____ A post-session debriefing is built in so you can conduct your own analysis of the session.

## Suggestions for Using the Diversity Training Planning Checklist

**Objectives:**
- Plan effective diversity training.
- Evaluate training once it has been conducted.

**Intended Audience:**
- Trainers charged with planning and implementing diversity training.
- Planning teams such as diversity task forces.

**Processing the Activity:**
- Individuals respond to the checklist, indicating those items that have been addressed in their planning.
- If the checklist is used as a planning tool, those items not checked can be attended to.
- If the checklist is used as an evaluation tool, those items not checked can be considered and plans for taking care of them before the next phase of training can be made.
- If the checklist is used by a group, those items not checked can be discussed and ways to include them in future training sessions can be planned.

**Questions for Discussion:**
- What aspects have we taken care of?
- What areas did we miss?
- How will/did these omissions in planning affect training?
- How can we take care of these aspects now?
- What will we do differently next time?

**Caveats and Considerations:**
- While this checklist serves as an effective self-evaluation tool for the trainer, the evaluation should not be done in a vacuum. Feedback from others—participants and/or co-planners—is important in getting a more complete assessment.

# Characteristics of an Effective Diversity Trainer

Heeding the caveats we've mentioned and following the suggestions at the end of the chapter will help you prepare successful workshops on this topic, but the most important element in diversity training is the trainer him/herself. The trainer is the tool, a critical element in effective training. While the central role of the trainer is acknowledged in any learning situation, the trainer-as-tool concept is even more important in diversity training and calls for additional skills and competencies. Take a look at *Characteristics of an Effective Diversity Trainer* to see how you stack up.

# Characteristics of an Effective Diversity Trainer

Directions: To assess your own competence and effectiveness as a diversity trainer, answer the following questions as honestly and accurately as possible.

| Questions | Almost Always | Sometimes | Almost Never |
|---|---|---|---|
| 1. My own life's issues around diversity sneak up on me. | ____ | ____ | ____ |
| 2. The most productive organizations or work groups are those in which no one feels left out. | ____ | ____ | ____ |
| 3. I understand the dimensions of culture that shape human behavior. | ____ | ____ | ____ |
| 4. I am able to present complex ideas simply and make them understood. | ____ | ____ | ____ |
| 5. I can accurately read a group's mood or tone. | ____ | ____ | ____ |
| 6. My own assumptions and stereotypes surprise me. | ____ | ____ | ____ |
| 7. It is stimulating to work with people who don't share my values. | ____ | ____ | ____ |
| 8. I can talk knowledgeably about the civil rights and other liberation movements. | ____ | ____ | ____ |
| 9. My energy keeps groups involved and attentive. | ____ | ____ | ____ |
| 10. I am comfortable confronting and negotiating with others. | ____ | ____ | ____ |
| 11. I find it difficult to keep my cool in the face of ideas that are offensive to me. | ____ | ____ | ____ |
| 12. I value a wide range of views and attitudes. | ____ | ____ | ____ |
| 13. I am a keen observer of human nature. | ____ | ____ | ____ |
| 14. I am comfortable speaking to groups of varying size and background. | ____ | ____ | ____ |
| 15. I can create a nonthreatening, high-trust learning environment. | ____ | ____ | ____ |
| 16. I'm in tune with my own biases. | ____ | ____ | ____ |
| 17. It bothers me to see people discounted because of age, gender, race, or any other diversity dimension. | ____ | ____ | ____ |
| 18. I continuously read and study up on contemporary issues related to the various groups represented in my organization. | ____ | ____ | ____ |
| 19. I am able to tell relevant anecdotes that hold people's interest. | ____ | ____ | ____ |
| 20. In high-conflict situations, I can facilitate discussion so that all viewpoints are aired. | ____ | ____ | ____ |
| 21. I carry no banner for any group or viewpoint. | ____ | ____ | ____ |
| 22. Diversity works when all sides make adaptations. | ____ | ____ | ____ |
| 23. Comparing cultural norms inside the United States and beyond its borders is interesting to me. | ____ | ____ | ____ |
| 24. I have effective techniques for dealing with disruptive participants. | ____ | ____ | ____ |
| 25. I can intervene at the appropriate time without making others feel threatened. | ____ | ____ | ____ |

Directions for Scoring: Score numbers 1, 6, and 11 first, and then record the score next to the corresponding number below.

1, 6, 11

Almost never = 4 points
Sometimes = 2 points
Almost always = 0 points

Then score the remaining 22 items by recording the score next to the appropriate number.

Almost always = 4 points
Sometimes = 2 points
Almost never = 0 points

| Trainer as Tool | Belief in Core Diversity Values | Content Knowledge |
|---|---|---|
| 1 _____ | 2 _____ | 3 _____ |
| 6 _____ | 7 _____ | 8 _____ |
| 11 _____ | 12 _____ | 13 _____ |
| 16 _____ | 17 _____ | 18 _____ |
| 21 _____ | 22 _____ | 23 _____ |

| Platform Skills | Facilitation Skills |
|---|---|
| 4 _____ | 5 _____ |
| 9 _____ | 10 _____ |
| 14 _____ | 15 _____ |
| 19 _____ | 20 _____ |
| 24 _____ | 25 _____ |

Scoring indicates:

| Points | |
|---|---|
| 80–100 | You're on the way to becoming an excellent diversity trainer. |
| 60–79 | You've got some of the pieces in place, but you need to work on developing your competence in certain areas. |
| 59 and below | Look at the key concepts measured here. If low scores are in platform and facilitation skills, development in these areas can greatly improve your competence. If knowledge is a low area, you can read and learn. If, however, low scores occur around core values, rethink your commitment to diversity training. Perhaps that's not the field of training for you. |

Question to consider:

1. What is your strong suit? Each category has a potential for 20 points. Which of the five is your highest?
2. Did you score zero points on any item? How about two points? Are these scores clustered in a particular category among the five?
3. Look at your low scores. What specific actions can you take to improve your diversity training based on the data you see here?

## Concepts Underlying Characteristics of an Effective Diversity Trainer

This questionnaire measures the trainer's ability in five areas that comprise effective diversity training. Below is an explanation of each.

1. **Trainer as tool.** This concept involves the trainer's awareness about how prejudice, stereotypes, assumptions—all the *isms* in general—affect him or her. Effective diversity training requires individual trainers with "no axes to grind": people who will not work through their personal issues on the participants in the group or get *hooked* by individuals who hold views offensive to the trainers.
2. **Belief in core diversity values.** Diversity training is built on a set of beliefs. Among those beliefs is the idea that diversity is an "inside job." This means we all need to find the comfort and security within ourselves to deal with differentness. Further, diversity implies inclusion, tolerance, adaptation, and equality. It is essential that any diversity trainer subscribe to these values.
3. **Content knowledge.** The body of knowledge found in diversity training requires some familiarity with theories drawn from anthropology, psychology, and sociology. It looks at human behavior in both groups and individuals. It also focuses on awareness of stereotypes and prejudice, culture as a primary shaper of behavior, and management skills adapted to heterogeneous, pluralistic organizations.
4. **Platform skills.** The ability to instruct, inspire, hold people's attention, provoke thought and discusion, and in general create a rich, stimulating, and results-oriented learning session depends largely on the trainer's ability in front of the group. Platform skills focus on presence and poise in training situations.
5. **Facilitation skills.** The ability to structure the group's processes and design an involving session around complex issues is a key facilitator skill. Further, an excellent facilitator affords dignity and respect to all participants and keeps the group on task while being flexible enough to change direction as needed. Facilitators, especially those in diversity training, need to create a safe, nonthreatening environment in which all ideas are heard.

# Suggestions for Using Characteristics of an Effective Diversity Trainer

**Objectives:**
- Identify the competencies critical for diversity training.
- Enable trainers, facilitators, and other HR professionals to assess their strengths and weaknesses in this field of training.

**Intended Audience:**
- HR professionals charged with training personnel to become diversity trainers within the organization (e.g., a train-the-trainer process).
- Internal and external consultants who deliver diversity training.
- HR professionals who need guidance in or guidelines for hiring external diversity consultants. This can furnish informal criteria.

**Processing the Activity:**
- Facilitators/trainers take the questionnaire and score it.
- If the questionnaire is administered to a group, the facilitator may list on an easel all participants' scores (omitting names) to show the range.
- The facilitator answers any questions about the items on the inventory and presents the ideas behind the five competencies being measured.
- Participants form into small groups or pairs and do an item analysis to assess their own strengths and weaknesses.
- The facilitator leads a large-group discussion to apply the learning.

**Questions for Discussion:**
- What are your greatest proficiencies?
- Where do you need the most improvement?
- Based on the identified competencies, do you foresee obstacles that may be difficult to overcome?
- What can you start doing today to shore up areas that need improvement?

**Caveats and Considerations:**
- The facilitator may do a group profile according to concept categories and assess strengths and weaknesses. Following this, the facilitator may ask, "What does this say we need to work on either as individual trainers or as a department?"

| Concept | High Score | Low Score |
|---|---|---|
| 1. | | |
| 2. | | |
| 3. | | |
| 4. | | |
| 5. | | |

This tool can be used to determine which facilitators would co-train most effectively together.

- Depending on the size of the group, the facilitator can close by asking questions such as
  1. What do you do best as a diversity trainer?
  2. What are you targeting for improvement?
  3. What one competency or improvement would make the greatest difference in your effectiveness?

# Suggestions for Diversity Training

Once you've utilized the previous checklists and considered the caveats, you are ready for a successful experience. We send you on your way with a few more hints that should help ensure a satisfying outcome for your efforts.

1.  **Create ground rules for your training.**  It is important to have a framework of acceptable behavior that all participants know, understand, and adhere to. These ground rules should be presented up front following the objectives. Keep them short, simple, and behaviorally focused. We have seen many facilitators present ground rules in their workshops; we have also seen groups create their own rules at the beginning of a session. In either case, here are a few frequently used examples of appropriate ground rules:
    - Speak for yourself.
    - Refrain from personal attacks.
    - Be open to new ideas.
    - Actively participate in the session.

2.  **Expect resistance.**  Many factors can influence the mindsets of participants in your training session. In one organization, we followed some diversity consultants who had triggered major blow-ups two years earlier. Although publicity prior to the session attempted to assure people this experience would be different, participants were skeptical, to say the least. They were resistant as they walked in the door, and one participant even refused to fill out his tent card. But we had done some homework. Knowing the background helped us anticipate participant reaction and prepare for the worst. The group eventually thawed, and resistance ultimately diminished. Expecting resistance got us through and made us less defensive. Anticipation can do the same for you.

3.  **Put diversity training in a larger, organizational context.**  Any diversity training that is treated like an accessory will never fit into the organizational life in a meaningful way, and its value and effectiveness will be short-lived. In some organizations, subtle discrimination persists and opportunities for advancement for women and people of color remain limited. In such cases, it is important that diversity training not only deal with how assumptions and stereotypes categorize and limit people (and how cross-cultural communication norms might influence a manager's perceptions of whom to hire or promote) but also focus on the organization's promotional and career development systems.

4.  **Help participants understand the role of socialization.**  Diveristy training is the most challenging and demanding work. Trainers are not just teaching new skills; we are looking at values, belief systems, and fundamental paradigms about how the world works and who is entitled to what. No other type

of training puts the core individual and all that he or she is so closely under the microscope. And in no other session are participants' values and belief systems, absorbed osmosis-like from infancy, under such tight scrutiny. It is often both startling and upsetting for people to have to dust off racist phrases learned from their parents or acknowledge early incidents of discrimination. The role of socialization stuns participants once they perceive it. Recently we taught a class that had twins, one male and one female. The young man had been programmed by his parents to go to college and get advanced degrees. His very bright sister was slotted—without her input—for marriage and parenting immediately after high school. That experience gave our attendees pause. It made all of us examine the personal programming we experienced about our own capabilities, as well as the messages we received about the expectations of other racial, gender, ethnic, or cultural groups.

5.  **Understand the complexity of the issues.**   Diversity-related issues are complex because so many norms, traditions, rituals, and values come under scrutiny. The study of cultures and subcultures is fascinating, but it is not easy because human nature tends to make us ethnocentric. Positive experiences and exposure to diverse people and groups can make us more tolerant of behavior different from our own. Just by looking at subcultures in the United States based on geography, race, and ethnicity, we can see that no one way is better than another; rather, all norms have both positive and negative value. The challenge is helping employees come to terms with the many variations coworkers bring to the organization or work team. Amid all this variety, it is important to create a common organizational culture whose goals, values, and expectations are strong enough to hold the group together.

6.  **Accept that the end result of diversity is a *fundamental* redistribution of resources and power.**   Coming to terms with this reality is not easy. Underlying most people's resistance is the perception that they will lose something in the transaction. Initially many participants in your training session may wish the new demographic trends would reverse themselves. As a diversity trainer, it is critical that you frame your concepts and discussion in a way that does not pit people and groups against each other and that enables participants to see what they stand to gain—or what they may lose if the status quo remains.

7.  **Make sure the person who champions your program has credibility and clout.**   Relegating the implementation or advocacy of the diversity program to someone invisible and unimportant in the organization consigns the training to a level of tokenism and insignificance. If you can't get top-level support, and if your efforts can't be assigned to someone who has respect and influence throughout the organization, that message will be broadcast loudly and clearly to all employees. Over the years, **the savvy troops have learned** what the CEO's pet projects are by who advocates and implements them. Similarly, they will know where diversity training ranks in importance when they learn who beats the drums for this program.

## Sample Training Agendas

Having done the necessary data gathering and planning, you are ready to structure your agenda and implement your training. The following sample agendas will guide you in structuring training sessions of various lengths, content, and objectives.

# Sample Agenda: Two-Hour Executive Briefing
# Understanding Diversity

| Time | Activity/Topic | Process |
|------|----------------|---------|
| 5 minutes | Introduction | |
| 5 minutes | Objectives: | Lecturette |
| | • Increase awareness and understanding about diversity and its impact on the organization. | |
| | • Generate support and commitment for the development of a diversity strategic plan. | |
| 20 minutes | Demographic Realities | Lecturette and discussion |
| | (OH 1–1 and other pertinent demographic statistics about the region and the organization) | |
| | Changes: | |
| | • In the work force | |
| | • In the region | |
| | • Within the organization | |
| | • Impact on the organization | |
| 30 minutes | Diversity = Business Imperative | Lecturette and discussion |
| | (OH 1–2 and information on the organization's own strategic plan) | |
| | • How dealing effectively with diversity is an advantage, increasing profitability, productivity, and survival. | |
| | • How diversity connects with the organization's strategic objectives. | |
| 30 minutes | Dimensions of diversity (OH 1–3): | Lecturette and discussion |
| | • Primary and secondary dimensions of diversity | |
| | • Identifying issues and obstacles that create barriers to teamwork, productivity, and morale | |
| | • Presentation of organizational audit data (from questionnaires, focus groups, and/or interviews), if available | |
| 25 minutes | Three levels of Managing Diversity (OH 8–4): | Lecturette and discussion |
| | • Explanation of three levels and the types of interventions (training, problem solving, etc.) appropriate for each. | |
| |    • Individual attitudes and beliefs | |
| |    • Management skills and practices | |
| |    • Organizational values and policies | |
| | • Where do we go from here? | |
| 5 minutes | Summary | Lecturette |

# Sample Agenda: Half-Day (3½-Hour) Diversity Awareness Session for Employees at all Levels

| Time | Activity/Topic | Process |
|---|---|---|
| 5 minutes | Introduction<br>• Purpose of the session<br>• Relevance of topic | Lecturette |
| 10 minutes | Warmup:<br>• What is the good news and bad news of working in a diverse environment? | Paired sharing<br>Facilitator solicits responses from group and charts responses. |
| 5 minutes | Objectives<br>• Increase awareness about workplace diversity.<br>• Increase comfort in dealing with others who are different. | Lecturette |
| 30 minutes | Dimensions of Diversity (OH 1–3):<br>• Explanation of the primary and secondary dimensions of diversity<br>• Impact of these differences on the job | Lecturette<br>Small-group discussion of the impact of these differences on the job<br>Facilitator then leads total group dicussion of major differences. |
| 10 minutes | Culture = Behavioral Software (OH 2–1) | Lecturette |
| 45 minutes | *You as a Culturally Diverse Entity* worksheet | Facilitator leads group brainstorming regarding sources of cultural programming and charts responses.<br>Individual worksheet<br>Paired sharing<br>Facilitator then leads total-group discussion of insights and learning. |
| 15 minutes | Break | |
| 15 minutes | Stereotypes and Prejudice | Lecturette<br>Facilitator then leads total-group discussion:<br>• Why do we make stereotypic judgments?<br>• How do they help/hurt?<br>• When have you been caught by your own stereotypic assumptions?<br>• When have you been the victim of stereotyping? |
| 50 minutes | *Stereotypes* worksheet | Individual worksheet<br>Small-group discussion<br>Facilitator leads total-group discussion of reactions and insights. |
| 10 minutes | Summary | Lecturette |
| 15 minutes | Closure<br>• What is the most important insight you gained from this session? | Paired sharing (or individual sharing with group) |

# Sample Agenda: Full-Day Management Skill-Building Session
# Skills for Managing a Diverse Staff

| Time | Activity/Topic | Process |
|------|----------------|---------|
| 5 minutes | Introduction | Lecturette |
| 15 minutes | Warm-up:<br>• Greatest challenges and greatest rewards in managing a diverse staff. | Paired sharing<br>Facilitator leads total-group sharing of responses. |
| 5 minutes | Objectives:<br>• Increase knowledge about the impact of diversity on work behavior.<br>• Gain skills in dealing effectively with staff of all backgrounds. | Lecturette |
| 15 minutes | Culture = Behavioral Software (OH 2–1) | Lecturette |
| 45 minutes | *You as a Culturally Diverse Entity* worksheet | Group brainstorming of sources of cultural programming: facilitator charts responses<br>Individual worksheet<br>Paired sharing<br>Facilitator then leads a total-group discussion of insights and learning |
| 15 minutes | Break | |
| 60 minutes | Ten Dimensions of Culture (OH 2–2)<br>*Dimensions of Culture* worksheet | Lecturette<br>In each of five small groups, participants identify cultural norms in the organization in 2 of the 10 dimensions. Then they identify behaviors that conflict with these norms.<br>Responses are charted on 10 flipchart sheets taped to the walls.<br>Each group then reports to the total group. |
| 20 minutes | *Analyzing Cultural Differences* worksheet | Individual worksheet<br>Paired sharing |
| 60 minutes | Lunch | |
| 10 minutes | Energizer<br>• "Most important piece of Feedback you ever got . . . | Paired sharing<br>Facilitator leads a total-group sharing of responses and themes. |
| 35 minutes | *Intercultural Feedback Skills* worksheet (OH 3–3) | Individual worksheet<br>Small-group sharing of feedback examples<br>Facilitator leads total-group discussion of reactions, difficulties, and learning. Then he/she asks each participant to write a feedback statement to make to an employee, using the skills learned. |

# Sample Agenda: Full-Day Management Skill-Building Session
## Skills for Managing a Diverse Staff (*Concluded*)

| Time | Activity/Topic | Process |
|---|---|---|
| 45 minutes | *Expected Employee Behaviors* worksheet | Group brainstorming of the most important behaviors participants expect from employees. |
| | | Faciltator charts responses. |
| | | Individuals then write responses on worksheet. |
| | | In small groups, participants discuss: |
| | | • Which behaviors are hardest to acquire? |
| | | • What cultural norms might be influencing the employee's behavior? |
| | | • How can you communicate these expectations to employees? |
| | | • What can you do to get more of the desired behaviors? |
| | | Facilitator leads total-group discussion of points made. |
| 15 minutes | Break | |
| 60 minutes | Resolving Conflicts: A Model of Cultural Synergy (OH 3–5) | Lecturette |
| | | In small groups, participants identify a real on-the-job example of diversity-related conflict. |
| | | The groups then use the model of cultural synergy to resolve it, charting their application of each of the three tips. |
| | | The groups report their analyses to the whole group. |
| 5 minutes | Summary | Lecturette |
| 15 minutes | Closure<br>"The skill I learned that I will use tomorrow is . . ." | Paired sharing |

# Sample Agenda: Full-Day Workshop (6 Hours)
# Opening Up the Promotional System

| Time | Activity/Topic | Process |
|------|----------------|---------|
| 10 minutes | Welcome/Introduction<br>Objectives:<br>• Gain awareness of subtle assumptions that impede your diversity promotion efforts.<br>• Determine what management characteristics are promoted in your company.<br>• Identify what the company needs to do to open up the promotion process.<br>• Make coaching a more active tool in opening up the promotion system. | Lecturette |
| 20 minutes | Warmup:<br>• What quality or skill do you possess that makes you highly promotable?<br>• What is the most important quality or skill you look for in promoting others? | Small-group discussion<br>In groups of four, participants discuss the two questions.<br>Then facilitator leads a discussion with the whole group, writing random answers on flipchart. |
| 20 minutes | *Valued Management Traits* worksheet<br>Participants fill out Section 1, "10 Most Important Traits") | Individual worksheet<br>Each individual lists the 10 most important traits the company values in promoting employees to a management position.<br>Facilitator leads group brainstorming and lists suggestions on flipchart.<br>Participants put a check mark by any of the 10 characteristics that describes them. Then the whole group discusses: What does this say about whom you hire or promote? Is it likely you'll hire someone like you? What is the implication of hiring or promoting your clone? |
| 10 minutes | Unconscious Factors That Influence Promotion (OH 10–1) | Lecturette<br>Group discussion<br>• Which of these factors has most influenced you?<br>• Which has created the biggest obstacle to having a more diverse staff? |

# Sample Agenda: Full-Day Workshop (6 Hours)
# Opening Up the Promotional System (*Continued*)

| Time | Activity/Topic | Process |
|---|---|---|
| 30 minutes | *Valued Management Traits* worksheet (cont'd) | Small-group discussion<br><br>Participants break into small discussion groups. Participants are asked to look at promotable qualities and answer four questions:<br><br>1. Which qualities are perceived to be male/female?<br><br>2. Which are valued in American business?<br><br>3. With which traits would people from other cultures, women, people of color, the differently abled, or persons of a different affectional orientation have difficulty?<br><br>4. What is the flip side of each of these characteristics? |
| 15 minutes | Break | |
| 30 minutes | *Valued Management Traits* worksheet (cont'd) | Facilitator leads whole-group discussion of the four questions dealt with in the small-group discussions. |
| 30 minutes | *Valued Management Traits*, Section 2<br>(List traits and answer question 1) | Each individual answers the questions on Section 2 of the worksheets. Participants go back to their small groups. They discuss the worksheet questions first. Then the whole group answers the questions:<br><br>• Who gets promoted?<br><br>• Who gets held back?<br><br>• What will this mean to the competitiveness of the organization?<br><br>• What are they willing to do differently? |
| 15 minutes | Summary:<br>• Tie group discussion to lecturette.<br>• Review morning. | Lecturette |
| 60 minutes | Lunch | |
| 15 minutes | Energizer: Great Coaches | Pairs brainstorm a list of coaches they admire and why. (They know them personally or admire them from afar.)<br><br>Paired sharing<br><br>Then facilitator makes two columns on flipchart and gets random responses from participants:<br><br>| Coach | Reason Admired |<br>|---|---|<br>| e.g., John Wooden | Won year after year got results; built character; demonstrated integrity | |

# Sample Agenda: Full-Day Workshop (6 Hours)
# Opening Up the Promotional System (*Concluded*)

| Time | Activity/Topic | Process |
|------|----------------|---------|
| 60 minutes | "What does your company do to increase promotions of its diverse employees?" (OH 10–3) | Individual worksheet<br>Small-group discussion:<br>Divide people into five groups by randomly counting off.<br>1. What is the organization's greatest strength in opening up the system?<br>2. What is its greatest weakness?<br>3. What needs to be done to expand the system?<br>Facilitator leads total-group discussion.<br>While participants are still in five groups, facilitator assigns one area of the questionnaire to each group. The five areas are:<br>1. Building connections<br>2. Political savvy<br>3. Dealing with multiple motivations<br>4. Positioning<br>5. Mastering change<br>On chart paper, each group comes up with concrete ideas to help potential supervisors and managers in one of these five areas. For example, "How can the organization help people build connections? (or become more politically savvy)?"<br>One person in each group reports ideas to whole group. |
| 15 minutes | Break | |
| 70 minutes | Coaching for Promotion | Small-group activity<br>Participants divide into seven groups. Information about each candidate is distributed.<br>Each group comes up with a coaching strategy and reports it to the whole group. (Strategies should be written on chart paper.)<br>Facilitator explains that the criteria and accomplishments of each person was the same; only the name and background differed.<br>With that new information, facilitator leads group discussion:<br>1. What differences in coaching exist?<br>2. On what factors are the differences based? What assumptions or expectations guide the coaching?<br>3. How can these differences be minimized so that some employees don't have less opportunity? |
| 10 minutes | Functions of a Cross-Cultural Coach (OH 10–4) | Lecturette |
| 10 minutes | Summary/Closure: "Most important learning I got from the day is . . ." | Quick response from each participant |

# Section II

## ACTIVITIES, WORKSHEETS, AND CHARTS

# Culture and You

If you woke up tomorrow morning and found that you belonged to another culture or ethnic group, how would your life be the same and how would it be different?

|  | Same | Different |
|---|---|---|
| 1. The friends you associate with |  |  |
| 2. The social activities you enjoy |  |  |
| 3. The foods you prefer |  |  |
| 4. The religion you practice |  |  |
| 5. The way you dress |  |  |
| 6. The community where you live |  |  |
| 7. The home you live in |  |  |
| 8. The job/position you hold |  |  |
| 9. The car you drive |  |  |
| 10. The music you enjoy listening to |  |  |
| 11. The language(s) you speak |  |  |
| 12. The political party you belong to |  |  |

# Suggestions for Using *Culture and You*

**Objectives:**

- To help individuals see the pervasiveness of cultural programming.
- To increase awareness about the interplay between culture and individual personality in influencing life situations.
- To empathize with individuals of other cultural backgrounds.

**Intended Audience:**

- Individuals seeking to increase their own awareness about cultural differences.
- Participants in diversity training sessions.
- Work group members coping with diversity-related issues.
- Staff dealing with customers/clients of other cultural backgrounds.

**Processing the Activity:**

- Individuals are asked to imagine themselves suddenly becoming members of another cultural or ethnic group in this society. Stress that they are to imagine being born into and socialized by that other culture. As a variation, individuals may be asked also to imagine themselves of a different gender, sexual preference, or physical ability level.
- Individuals discuss reactions and insights in pairs, triads, or small groups.
- Smaller groupings share discussion highlights with a total group in a wrap-up discussion.

**Questions for Discussion:**

- Which parts of your life would remain the same? Which would be different?
- On what did you base your decisions about where to place your checks?
- What surprises did you have? What reactions?
- What questions or issues does this raise for you?
- What did you learn from this activity?

**Caveats and Considerations:**

- Some individuals may balk at being asked to make choices based on assumptions or stereotypes. This activity can lead to a discussion of such issues.
- When giving directions, be sure to emphasize that the purpose of the activity is not to reinforce stereotypes, but to see how culture influences our lives.
- Issues beyond culture, such as income or education level, will undoubtedly be brought up as influences. This serves to broaden the scope of the discussion to other dimensions of diversity.

# How I Like to Be Treated

Check off any of these statements that are true for you. Feel free to add more of your own as well.

_____ "I want to be told when I make a mistake so I don't make it again."

_____ "I want you to tell me if you disagree with me."

_____ "I like being told when I'm doing well so I know I'm on the right track."

_____ "I want the boss to ask for my input and to listen to my concerns."

_____ "I want the freedom to do things my own way."

_____ "I want my boss to roll up his/her sleeves and help out when we're busy."

_____ "I don't want to have to ask for directions and approval every step of the way."

_____ "I like it when others tell me what's on their minds."

_____ "I like it when people call me by my first name."

_____ "I want my staff to see me as their partner rather than as their boss."

_____ "It feels good when I am noticed and singled out for praise."

_____ "I like to be seen as an individual, not just considered one of the group."

_____ "I like being treated as an equal."

_____ "I like people to look at me in the eye when they talk to me."

_____ "I like _____ ."

_____ "It feels good when _____ ."

## Suggestions for Using *How I Like to Be Treated*

**Objectives:**

- To identify one's own behavioral preferences and expectations of others.
- To increase awareness of the cultural influences on those preferences.
- To empathize with those who hold different expectations.

**Intended Audience:**

- Individuals wanting to increase their own sensitivity to cultural differences.
- Trainees in diversity seminars.
- Managers desiring better communication and relationships with diverse employees.
- Work-group members attempting to overcome cultural obstacles in work relationships.

**Processing the Activity:**

- Ask individuals to check their own preferences, adding others if desired.
- Have individuals jot down their typical reactions to not being treated as desired.
- Discuss, in small groups or together as a whole group, how culture influences these preferences.
- Ask individuals to share "war stories" about examples of differences in preferences.
- Lead group discussion of the consequences for individuals and work relationships when individuals do not give or get the desired treatment.

**Questions for Discussion:**

- Which did you check? Which did you not check?
- How/where did you acquire these preferences?
- Which are part of the mainstream culture of your organization?
- What happens if you don't get the behavior you want? How do you feel? How do you react?
- What does this tell you about dealing with and managing diverse individuals?

**Caveats and Considerations:**

- To avoid arguments and polarization over which of these behaviors are *right* or *better,* explain that they are individual preferences. It is important to recognize them so we can clearly communicate expectations and so we can avoid judging others who act otherwise and have different expectations.

# You as a Culturally Diverse Entity

Directions: In each circle write one of the sources of your cultural programming. Then next to each circle write the most important rules, norms, and values you learned from that source.

1.  What reactions to and/or surprises do you have regarding your own cultural diversity?

2.  Do any of your cultural programs come in conflict with one another? If so, where?

## Suggestions for Using *You as a Culturally Diverse Entity*

**Objectives:**

- To identify the sources of one's own cultural programming.
- To see oneself as a microcosm of the societal dynamic of intercultural contact.
- To increase awareness about the complexity of each individual's cultural programming, which in turn affects behavior.
- To raise awareness about the need to find out more about the backgrounds of others in the workplace.
- To understand that everyone has a culture.
- To learn more about others with whom one works in order to increase understanding.

**Intended Audience:**

- Individuals wanting to increase their understanding and awareness about cultural influences and intercultural interactions on the job.
- Trainees in diversity seminars.
- Members of work teams wanting to understand each other better.
- Managers wanting to learn more about employees.

**Processing the Activity:**

- Have the group brainstorm sources of cultural programming and chart responses on an easel or a board. You might get them going by asking them how they learned the rules of behavior they now live by.
- Individuals write one source of their own cultural programming in each circle on the diagram. Next to each, they write the most important rules, norms, and values they learned.
- Individuals, in pairs or small groups, share information from their circles. They then discuss their reactions and the implications of the information.
- Total group discussion of reactions, insights, and learning.

**Questions for Discussion:**

- Which were the most important sources of your programming?
- Where do they come in conflict?
- Under what circumstances does one take priority over another?
- How are these differences resolved?
- What similarities and differences did you find with your partner(s) in your discussion group?
- What do you know about the programming of your colleagues, staff members, bosses, and so on? How can you find out more?
- What insight did you get?
- What does this say about dealing with others who are different from you?

**Caveats and Considerations:**

- This activity causes participants to look back to childhood, which can be a painful or emotional experience for some. It is not surprising to see tear-filled eyes as individuals share their experiences and memories with others in the room.
- Tell people at the beginning of the activity that they will be sharing their diagram with another person or a small group. In this way individuals can control the degree of disclosure.

# Comparing Cultural Norms and Values

| Aspects of Culture | Mainstream American Culture | Other Cultures |
|---|---|---|
| 1. Sense of self and space | Informal<br>Handshake | Formal<br>Hugs, bows, handshakes |
| 2. Communication and language | Explicit, direct communication<br>Emphasis on content—<br>meaning found in words | Implicit, indirect communication<br>Emphasis on context—<br>meaning found around words |
| 3. Dress and appearance | "Dress for success" ideal<br>Wide range in accepted dress | Dress seen as a sign of position, wealth, prestige<br>Religious rules |
| 4. Food and eating habits | Eating as a necessity—fast food | Dining as a social experience<br>Religious rules |
| 5. Time and time consciousness | Linear and exact time consciousness<br>Value on promptness—<br>time = money | Elastic and relative time consciousness<br>Time spent on enjoyment of relationships |
| 6. Relationships, family, friends | Focus on nuclear family<br>Responsibility for self<br>Value on youth, age seen as handicap | Focus on extended family<br>Loyalty and responsibility to family<br>Age given status and respect |
| 7. Values and norms | Individual orientation<br>Independence<br>Preference for direct confrontation of conflict | Group orientation<br>Conformity<br>Preference for harmony |
| 8. Beliefs and attitudes | Egalitarian<br>Challenging of authority<br>Individuals control their destiny<br>Gender equity | Hierarchical<br>Respect for authority and social order<br>Individuals accept their destiny<br>Different roles for men and women |
| 9. Mental processes and learning style | Linear, logical, sequential<br>Problem-solving focus | Lateral, holistic, simultaneous<br>Accepting of life's difficulties |
| 10. Work habits and practices | Emphasis on task<br>Reward based on individual achievement<br>Work has intrinsic value | Emphasis on relationships<br>Rewards based on seniority, relationships<br>Work is a necessity of life |

Source: Adapted from Philip R. Harris and Robert T. Moran, *Managing Cultural Differences*, 2nd ed. (Houston: Gulf Publishing, 1987).

# Dimensions of Culture

The following chart gives you an opportunity to make some notes about cultural differences you
have encountered in each of the 10 areas of cultural programming.

| **Dimensions of Culture** | **Examples of Differences** |
|---|---|
| 1. Sense of self and space | |
| • Distance | _____ |
| • Touch | _____ |
| • Formal/informal | _____ |
| • Open/closed | _____ |
| 2. Communication and language | |
| • Language/dialect | _____ |
| • Gestures/expressions/tone | _____ |
| • Direct/indirect | _____ |
| 3. Dress and appearance | |
| • Clothing | _____ |
| • Hair | _____ |
| • Grooming | _____ |
| 4. Food and eating habits | |
| • Food restrictions/taboos | _____ |
| • Utensils/hands | _____ |
| • Manners | _____ |
| 5. Time and time consciousness | |
| • Promptness | _____ |
| • Age/status | _____ |
| • Pace | _____ |
| 6. Relationships | |
| • Family | _____ |
| • Age/gender/kindred | _____ |
| • Status | _____ |
| 7. Values and norms | |
| • Group vs. individual | _____ |
| • Independence vs. conformity | _____ |
| • Privacy | _____ |
| • Respect | _____ |
| • Competition vs. cooperation | _____ |
| 8. Beliefs and attitudes | |
| • Religion | _____ |
| • Position of women | _____ |
| • Social order/authority | _____ |
| 9. Mental processes and learning | |
| • Left/right brain emphasis | _____ |
| • Logic/illogic | _____ |
| 10. Work habits and practices | |
| • Work ethic | _____ |
| • Rewards/promotions | _____ |
| • Status of type of work | _____ |
| • Division of labor/organization | _____ |

Source: Adapted from Philip R. Harris and Robert T. Moran, *Managing Cultural Differences*, 2nd ed. (Houston: Gulf Publishing, 1987).

## Suggestions for Using *Dimensions of Culture*

**Objectives:**

- Identify both mainstream and other cultural norms.
- Recognize the cultural roots of behaviors encountered at work.
- Expand understanding and knowledge of different cultural norms.

**Intended Audience:**

- Individuals wanting to increase their knowledge about different cultural norms.
- Trainees in a diversity seminar.
- Employees wanting to understand and deal more effectively with individuals (staff, customers, or clients) from other cultures.

**Processing the Activity:**

- During a lecturette on the information on the preceding pages regarding different cultural norms in the 10 areas of programming, individuals make notes on the chart.
- Group is divided into smaller groups, with each discussing one or two of the areas of programming and sharing differences and their impact in the workplace. Information is charted on a flip chart or board.
- Small groups report to the larger group, giving a recap of the points made in their discussion.

**Questions for Discussion:**

- What are mainstream norms in each area? Norms of other cultures?
- What are the norms in your organization?
- Which differences cause problems or misunderstanding?

**Caveats and Considerations:**

- It may be difficult for individuals to see the cultural influence beneath the behaviors. You may need to help by giving additional examples or asking participants from other cultures to share examples.
- It is important to avoid giving the impression that people from other cultures are so different, and that other norms are so strange, that we cannot understand them. One way is to present sets of differences as a continuum, for example, conformity ↔ individualism. Peer pressure and group solidarity are powerful shapers of behaviors in mainstream America, and in cultures that value conformity, individuals do have their own opinions and may want the freedom to do things their own way.
- It is also important to avoid creating new stereotypes about different cultural groups. It can be insightful to have individuals from the same culture discuss how differently they interpret their own culture's norms. The group then sees that all those of a particular group (African-Americans, Cambodians, Russians, Israelis, etc.) are not the same and that there are as many differences within a group as from group to group.
- This activity can also be expanded by having the group identify mainstream norms using popular sayings and aphorisms, for example:

    *Better late than never, but better never late.*

    *A penny saved is a penny earned.*

    *You are your brother's keeper.*

    —which express cultural values.

# Analyzing Cultural Differences

Apply what you just read about different cultural programming to your own situation. Choose one of your employees whose cultural programming is different from yours. (You'll get more from this analysis if you choose an individual with whom you are experiencing difficulties.) Analyze your own programming first, in each of the 10 areas; then analyze what you think your employee's programming has been.

See if you can identify any of the areas where differences in programming and expectations may be causing some rubs. How can you use this information to help you overcome some of these cultural barriers? Perhaps you will see and interpret this employee's behavior differently now, so it will not irritate you quite as much. Or maybe you can explain your own behavior to the employee to clear up misunderstandings and erroneous assumptions. Better still, can you negotiate a resolution by each of you giving a little and creating a new norm you both can live with?

| Aspects of Culture | Employee | You |
|---|---|---|
| 1. Sense of self and space | | |
| 2. Communication and language | | |
| 3. Dress and appearance | | |
| 4. Food and eating habits | | |
| 5. Time and time consciousness | | |
| 6. Relationships, family, friends | | |
| 7. Values and norms | | |
| 8. Beliefs and attitudes | | |
| 9. Mental processes and learning style | | |
| 10. Work habits and practices | | |

Source: Adapted from Philip R. Harris and Robert T. Moran, *Managing Cultural Differences*, 2nd ed. (Houston: Gulf Publishing, 1987).

# Suggestions for Using *Analyzing Cultural Differences*

**Objectives:**

- Apply information about cultural programming to specific work relationships.
- Identify cultural differences that may be at the root of performance problems or communication barriers.
- Gain more information and a new perspective that can help in resolving interpersonal issues on the job.

**Intended Audience:**

- Managers wanting to improve their relationship with, resolve a conflict with, or increase commitment from a specific employee or a group of employees from a similar background.
- Managers participating in a managing diversity seminar.
- Employees needing to increase effectiveness with customers/clients from other cultures.
- Employees wanting to resolve a conflict with someone from another cultural background.

**Processing the Activity:**

- Individuals jot down information about their own cultural programming in each of the 10 areas, then about the programming of one of their employees (or customers/clients, or co-workers).
- Individuals analyze differences at the heart of the problem.
- Individuals share their analyses in pairs or small groups, getting input from their partner(s) and responding to the discussion questions.
- Total group shares insights gained.

**Questions for Discussion:**

- What are the most irritating differences?
- What are the advantages and disadvantages of your norms, rules, and values? The other individuals'?
- What does this analysis tell you that can help you resolve this problem?
- What are you willing to do or expect differently in order to resolve this? What do you need to ask the other individual to do or expect differently?

**Caveats and Considerations:**

- Occasionally, individuals are so emotionally involved in an interpersonal impasse that it is difficult for them to stand back and analyze it more objectively. You can help them by offering some examples of differences that may be operating.

# Cross-Cultural Hooks

Another way to help get beyond irritations you may feel when encountering cultural differences is to identify the specific behaviors that bother you and then look deeper to understand the cultural programming that underlies them. Using the following cross-cultural hook list will help you do that.

   Put a check by any of the cross-cultural hooks that could result in frustration or negative interactions between you and another individual.
Then, next to any you've checked, jot down your reaction when you encounter this hook.

☐   Discounting or refusing to deal with women.

☐   Speaking in a language other than English.

☐   Bringing whole family/children to appointments.

☐   Refusal to shake hands with women.

☐   No nonverbal feedback (lack of facial expression).

☐   No eye contact.

☐   Soft, "dead fish" handshake.

☐   Standing too close when talking.

☐   Heavy accent or limited English facility.

☐   Coming late to appointments.

☐   Withholding or not volunteering necessary information.

☐   Not taking initiative to ask questions.

☐   Calling/not calling you by your first name.

☐   Emphasizing formal titles in addressing people.

☐   Other: _____ .

What aspects of cultural programming are at the root of this behavior?

# Suggestions for Using *Cross-Cultural Hooks*

**Objectives:**

- Identify personal cross-cultural button pushers.
- Recognize the cultural sources of irritating behaviors.
- Take a first step in getting beyond culturally connected blocks to productive relationships.

**Intended Audience:**

- Individuals seeking to increase cross-cultural understanding.
- Trainees in a diversity seminar.
- Managers who are finding difficulties in dealing with their diverse staff members.
- Employees who are experiencing negative interactions with other employees and/or customers/clients of other cultures.

**Processing the Activity:**

- Individuals check those behaviors they find irritating. Then they jot down their typical reaction to each behavior checked.
- After a lecturette or explanation of the 10 dimensions of culture, individuals discuss in small groups or total group the dimensions of culture that may be at the source of each behavior checked.
- Individuals discuss insights or new perspectives gained.

**Questions for Discussion:**

- What are your typical reactions when you get hooked?
- How does this affect how you deal with the situation?
- Which areas of cultural programming come into play?
- What are you willing to do to adapt to a particular norm?
- What are you willing to do to teach others to adapt to a particular norm?

# Decreasing Ethnocentrism

|  | Disadvantages | Advantages |
|---|---|---|
| **American Cultural Norms** | | |
| 1. Emphasis on promptness and time | _____ | _____ |
| 2. Direct explicit communication | _____ | _____ |
| 3. Competitive spirit | _____ | _____ |
| 4. Rugged individualism | _____ | _____ |
| 5. Informality in relationships | _____ | _____ |

|  | Advantages | Disadvantages |
|---|---|---|
| **Other Cultural Norms** | | |
| 1. Emphasis on harmony and order | _____ | _____ |
| 2. Respect for authority | _____ | _____ |
| 3. Precedence of group over the individual | _____ | _____ |
| 4. Focus on relationship building | _____ | _____ |
| 5. Emphasis on saving face | _____ | _____ |

# Suggestions for Using *Decreasing Ethnocentrism*

**Objectives:**

- To see cultural norms in a less ethnocentric, more neutral light.
- To increase open-mindedness in encountering different norms.

**Intended Audience:**

- Individuals seeking increased cultural sensitivity.
- Managers frustrated with behaviors arising from different cultural norms.
- Employees frustrated with behaviors of co-workers or clients/customers that arise from different cultural norms.
- Trainees in diversity seminars.

**Processing the Activity:**

- Individually or in groups, list the advantages of both mainstream American and other cultures' norms.
- Discuss reactions, surprises, and insights gained.
- As a personal application, individuals identify a particular norm they find difficult. They follow the same process, listing advantages and disadvantages of that norm.

**Questions for Discussion:**

- Which norms were hard to find either advantages or disadvantages for?
- Which norms do you feel strongest about?
- What surprises did you have? What insights?
- How can this help you in dealing with differences on the job?

**Caveats and Considerations:**

- Individuals may want to get into discussions about the *rightness* and/or *wrongness* of particular norms. Avoid polarization by reminding them that while they may have preferences, all cultural norms cut two ways and that working with others who have different norms is made much easier when we approach them without the judgments that their ways are wrong or inferior.
- As a variation, groups may make their own lists of favorite American norms and irritating foreign norms.

# Stereotypes

Check any of the following assumptions and beliefs you have held about other cultures or ethnic groups. Also check any you have heard, though not thought yourself. Then identify the group. Finally, write the name of an individual who disproves the stereotype.

|  |  |  | Group | Disprove |
|---|---|---|---|---|
| _____ | 1. | Are smart and work hard | _____ | _____ |
| _____ | 2. | Are very good at sports | _____ | _____ |
| _____ | 3. | Tend to keep to themselves | _____ | _____ |
| _____ | 4. | Are usually good dancers | _____ | _____ |
| _____ | 5. | Are lazy, don't work hard, and aren't reliable | _____ | _____ |
| _____ | 6. | Usually become rich by cheating others | _____ | _____ |
| _____ | 7. | Are sneaky and not trustworthy | _____ | _____ |
| _____ | 8. | Are uninsured and don't have driver's licenses | _____ | _____ |
| _____ | 9. | Are dirty and smell bad | _____ | _____ |
| _____ | 10. | Are uneducated and not very intelligent | _____ | _____ |
| _____ | 11. | Are associated with organized crime | _____ | _____ |
| _____ | 12. | Think they are better than others | _____ | _____ |
| _____ | 13. | Don't want to become American | _____ | _____ |
| _____ | 14. | Are aggressive and pushy | _____ | _____ |
| _____ | 15. | Talk and think only about making money | _____ | _____ |
| _____ | 16. | Are happy-go-lucky and easy-going | _____ | _____ |
| _____ | 17. | Laugh and smile a lot | _____ | _____ |
| _____ | 18. | Don't want to learn English | _____ | _____ |
| _____ | 19. | Have illegitimate children | _____ | _____ |
| _____ | 20. | Can't hold their liquor and drink too much | _____ | _____ |
| _____ | 21. | Do well in school and get advanced degrees | _____ | _____ |
| _____ | 22. | Make good gardeners | _____ | _____ |
| _____ | 23. | Make the neighborhood go downhill | _____ | _____ |
| _____ | 24. | Are bigoted, prejudiced, and biased | _____ | _____ |
| _____ | 25. | Are miserly and ungenerous | _____ | _____ |

# Suggestions for Using *Stereotypes*

## Objectives:

- Becoming aware of and admitting one's own stereotypes.
- Recognizing the pervasiveness of these preconceived assumptions in society.
- Taking steps to overcome stereotypic and prejudicial thinking.

## Intended Audience:

- Individuals who want to increase sensitivity in dealing with others different from them.
- Managers who work with diverse groups.
- Trainees at a diversity awareness and cultural sensitivity seminar.
- Employees needing to deal more sensitively with individuals from diverse groups.

## Processing the Activity:

- Individuals check any stereotype they have held or heard. They then write the group about which each one checked is said. Then they write the name of an individual from their own experience who disproves this stereotype.
- Individuals discuss their responses in pairs or small groups, and their reactions and insights as well.
- Total group discusses reactions and insights.

## Questions for Discussion:

- What was your reaction to doing this activity?
- What surprises did you have?
- Where do these assumptions come from?
- How do they impact your behavior at work?
- What can you do to overcome this kind of thinking?
- How can you respond when you hear stereotypic comments?

## Caveats and Considerations:

- Tell participants before they begin that they will be sharing their response with others.
- Expect tension and nervous laughter, as this activity is uncomfortable for most people. Discuss these feelings when processing the activity.
- Individuals apply the activity by listing the diverse groups they work with, the assumptions they hold about these groups, and finally examples which disprove the assumptions.

# Lexicon of appropriate terms

| When Referring to | Use | Instead of |
|---|---|---|
| Women | Women | Girls, ladies, gals, females |
| Black people | African-Americans, Caribbean-Americans, black people, people of color | Negroes, minorities |
| Asian people | Asian-Americans, Japanese, Koreans, Pakistanis, etc.; differentiate between foreign nationals and American born; people of color | Minorities |
| Pacific Islanders | Pacific Islanders, Polynesians, Maoris, etc.; use island name, e.g., Cook Islanders, Hawaiians; people of color | Asians, minorities |
| American Indians | American Indians, Native Americans; name of tribe, e.g., Navajo, Iroquois; people of color | Minorities |
| People of Hispano-Latin-American origin | Latinas/Latinos, Chicanas/Chicanos; use country of national origin, e.g., Cubanos, Puerto Ricans, Chileans; people of color; Hispanics | Minorities, Spanish-surnamed |
| Gay men and lesbians | Gay men, lesbians | Homosexuals |
| Differently abled people | Differently abled, developmentally disabled, physically disabled, physically challenged | Handicapped, crippled |
| White people | European-Americans; use country of national origin, e.g., Irish-Americans, Polish-Americans; white people | Anglos, WASPs |
| Older/younger adults | Older adults, elderly, younger people, young adults | Geriatrics, kids, yuppies |

Source: Marilyn Loden and Judy Losener, *Workforce America! Managing Employee Diversity as a Vital Resource.* (Burr Ridge, Il.: Irwin Professional Publishing, 1991).

# Intercultural Feedback Skills

**1.  Make observations about behaviors and conditions, not judgments about the person.**

| Judgment/Evaluation | Behavior/Situation |
|---|---|
| a.  This report is incomplete. | *I'd like to see a table of contents and summary added.* |
| b.  Your tardiness has become a problem. | _____ |
| c.  Your work area is sloppy. | _____ |
| d.  I'd like more professional behavior from office staff. | _____ |
| e.  I've heard complaints about your attitude. | _____ |

**2.  Use the passive rather than the active voice.**

| Active | Passive |
|---|---|
| a.  You forgot to turn off the air conditioner. | *The air conditioner was left on all night.* |
| b.  You made some errors in these computations. | _____ |
| c.  You are late from lunch again. | _____ |
| d.  The night shift left these charts incomplete. | _____ |
| e.  Your department is slow in returning these forms. | _____ |

**3.  Be positive, telling what you do want, not what you don't.**

| Negative | Positive |
|---|---|
| a.  That's not the way to do that. | *Try it this way.* |
| b.  Don't be late to the meeting. | _____ |
| c.  Don't forget that your time cards are due on Thursdays now. | _____ |
| d.  There's not enough initiative on this staff. | _____ |
| e.  You're not following procedures. | _____ |

## Suggestions for Using *Intercultural Feedback Skills*

**Objectives:**

- To practice three specific feedback techniques useful in intercultural communication.
- To develop additional feedback skills that can prevent loss of face.

**Intended Audience:**

- Managers wanting to gain additional skill in giving feedback to diverse employees.
- Trainees in a managing diversity seminar.
- Trainers wanting to gain additional skill in giving feedback to diverse trainees.

**Processing the Activity:**

- After reading the section *Ten Ways to Provide Feedback without Loss of Face* or hearing a lecturette on the topic, individuals write their own feedback statements for each of the three techniques.
- Then, if in a group, they can form smaller groups to share their statements, giving each other feedback on them. If working individually, compare statements to the suggestions at the end of the chapter.
- Total group then discusses difficulties encountered and learning from this activity.
- To apply the learning, individuals using situations from their own experience write three feedback statements, one for each technique, which they would give in their real-life situation.

**Questions for Discussion:**

- Which techniques were easiest? Most difficult?
- Where could you use these?

**Caveats and Considerations:**

- Some individuals may feel disgruntled because techniques 1 and 3 are standard feedback skills suggested in many supervisory and management development programs. Acknowledging their previous training in these areas up front may help circumvent this potential resistance. Stress that while it is an *old* technique, it has value with this *new* issue.
- Technique 2, using passive language, is apt to be difficult for native English speakers. There may be resistance from those who see it as vague, beating around the bush, and avoiding the issue. Help individuals see that it is an additional technique they may choose to use or not to use when and if appropriate.

# Intercultural Feedback Checklist
# for Managers

Think of a recent feedback situation in which you gave feedback to an employee from a different background. Check each of the techniques you used in that process.

_____   1.  I positioned the feedback as a benefit to the receiver.

_____   2.  I built a relationship first.

_____   3.  I went from subtle to more direct communication.

_____   4.  I made observations about behaviors and conditions, not judgments about the person.

_____   5.  I used the passive rather than the active voice.

_____   6.  I was positive, telling what I wanted, not what I didn't want.

_____   7.  I gave the feedback to the group rather than to individuals.

_____   8.  I gave feedback in a low-key and private way.

_____   9.  I used an intermediary.

_____   10. I assured the individual of my respect for him/her.

## Suggestions for Using the *Intercultural Feedback Checklist for Managers*

**Objectives:**

- To become aware of additional feedback techniques that could be employed.
- To identify feedback techniques utilized.
- To help managers plan more effective approaches for future feedback giving.

**Intended Audience:**

- Managers wanting to overcome cultural barriers in giving feedback to employees.
- Trainees in a managing diversity seminar.
- Trainers wanting to overcome cultural barriers in giving feedback to trainees.

**Processing the Activity:**

- Individuals analyze recent feedback-giving experience by checking which of the 10 techniques they used.
- In pairs or small groups they discuss their satisfaction with their feedback session, which techniques were used, and which could have been used to make the feedback even more effective. (If working alone, these same issues can be considered.)
- Large group discussion of insights, learning, and application.

**Questions for Discussion:**

- How satisfied were you with effectiveness of your feedback giving?
- Which techniques did you use? Which did you not use?
- Which might have helped make the feedback giving more effective?
- What would you do differently the next time you give feedback to diverse employees?

**Caveats and Considerations:**

- This activity can also be used as a planning guide for future feedback giving.

# Expected Employee Behaviors

Place a check mark next to those behaviors you expect of your staff. Then go back and place an X next to those behaviors you have a difficult time getting.

I expect employees to . . .

### Time

_____ Be on time for work, meetings, appointments.

_____ Be prompt in returning from breaks.

_____ Be responsible for their own time, taking breaks and lunch when needed.

_____ Give early notification of absences due to illness.

_____ Stick to assigned break and lunch times.

_____ Give requests for vacation time in advance.

_____ Meet deadlines on projects and tasks.

_____ Give advance notification of deadlines that can't be met.

_____ Other: _____.

### Taking Initiative and Solving Problems

_____ Suggest improvements and solutions.

_____ Participate in staff meetings by discussing and sharing.

_____ Work together to find solutions to problems.

_____ Take independent action to deal with problems, then tell me about it.

_____ Use good judgment about when to ask me before they take independent action.

_____ When carrying out delegated tasks, check in with me as planned.

_____ Other: _____.

### Announcing Problems and Giving ''Bad News''

_____ Let me know when there's a problem so we can fix it.

_____ Tell me when they disagree.

_____ Let me know when they are having difficulty.

_____ Tell me about complaints from clients/customers.

_____ Let me know when a mistake has been made.

_____ Other: _____.

### Communication

_____ Let me know when something is unclear or confusing.

_____ Ask if they don't understand.

_____ Speak English on the job.

_____ Make no derogatory remarks about another group.

_____ Not speak another language around others who do not understand.

_____ Other: _____.

# Suggestions for Using *Expected Employee Behaviors*

## Objectives:

• Identify behaviors expected of employees.
• Pinpoint those that are forthcoming and those that are not.

## Intended Audience:

• Managers wanting to increase productivity, follow-through, and commitment of staff.
• Trainees in a managing diversity seminar.

## Processing the Activity:

• Individuals check those behaviors they expect of employees, then go back and place an X next to those they have difficulty getting.
• In groups, individuals share their checklists and discuss those behaviors that are most difficult to get from staff. They then discuss ways to get the desired behaviors from staff.
• Individuals make a commitment to take specific action to get the desired behavior(s).

## Questions for Discussion:

• Which behaviors are hardest to get from employees?
• What might be the cultural norms influencing employees' behavior?
• How can you communicate these expectations to employees?
• What can you do to get more of the desired behaviors?

## Caveats and Considerations:

• This tool can be used by HR professionals or employee relations specialists in coaching managers to more effective behavior.
• This tool can also be used in general supervisory/management training courses.

Once you have identified which behaviors you want, as well as those you are and are not getting, you need to figure out how you can teach these American cultural expectations to your staff. Explaining the reason for the behavior's desirability is important in this process. For example, you may say,

• "It may sound odd, but I like 'bad news.' I want to know when something goes wrong so we can fix it as soon as possible. If no one tells me, I'm not able to do my job, which is to solve problems that get in the way of productivity."
• "When you participate in staff meetings and make suggestions about improvements, that shows me you take your job seriously and are a committed employee."
• "Being on time for meetings shows you respect others' time."
• "Speaking a language that others do not understand makes them feel left out. It may also make them angry and resentful."

# Sample Responses for Exercises

**Giving Directions**

- **Be specific and explicit.**

  a. *Take this to environmental engineering in B-36 and tell them to fix the broken switch.*

  b. *Requests for vacations and time off during November and December must be turned in by 9:00 A.M. tomorrow.*

  c. *Drop these off at the mailroom slot on your way out.*

**Giving Feedback**

- **Make observations about behaviors and conditions, not judgments about the person.**

  b. *You need to be at your work station by 8:00 A.M. each day.*

  c. *I'd like the work area clear of food and coffee cups.*

  d. *I'd like the phones answered by the third ring with "Good morning/afternoon, data processing, this is Teresa."*

  e. *I'd like customers greeted with a smile and treated like a guest in your home.*

- **Use the passive rather than the active voice.**

  b. *There are a few errors in these computations.*

  c. *The desk was uncovered for a half hour this afternoon.*

  d. *These charts were found incomplete this morning.*

  e. *These forms have been turned in late for the last three weeks.*

- **Be positive, telling what you do want, not what you don't.**

  b. *I'd like to start the meeting promptly at 9:00.*

  c. *Please remember to turn in time cards on Thursdays now.*

  d. *I'd like to see people offering to help each other when their own work is done.*

  e. *I'd like you to follow the steps outlined in the personnel manual when calling in sick.*

# Team Effectiveness Checklist

There are 15 questions, and all you need to do is respond by putting a check in the appropriate column.

| Symptoms | Yes | No |
|---|---|---|
| 1. Our team (or task force) has clearly defined objectives. | ____ | ____ |
| 2. Expectations of how we are going to operate have been collectively determined. | ____ | ____ |
| 3. An effective mechanism exists for dealing with interpersonal and/or intercultural conflict. | ____ | ____ |
| 4. Group trust builds because people come through on their commitments. | ____ | ____ |
| 5. Group members help each other out when needed. | ____ | ____ |
| 6. Team members can talk easily about joys and frustrations on the job. | ____ | ____ |
| 7. There is usually an absence of competition between members of our team. | ____ | ____ |
| 8. Effective processes exist for solving both system and interpersonal problems. | ____ | ____ |
| 9. Cultural differences such as time consciousness are acknowledged and dealt with. | ____ | ____ |
| 10. Our mission statement has been discussed and jointly agreed upon. | ____ | ____ |
| 11. The values we preach are the values we practice. | ____ | ____ |
| 12. There is a strong belief in our mutual purpose and interdependence. | ____ | ____ |
| 13. Each person on the team is clear about everyone's job. | ____ | ____ |
| 14. *Nonjudgmental* is a word that accurately describes the attitude toward differentness on this team. | ____ | ____ |
| 15. Official communication is more reliable than the grapevine. | ____ | ____ |

## Suggestions for Using the *Team Effectiveness Checklist*

### Objectives:

- Enable team members to assess their collective effectiveness.
- Determine areas where the team needs strengthening.
- Gain awareness about how individual team members view the strength and weakness of the team.

### Intended Audience:

- Managers to use with their own work groups.
- Internal and external training professionals who conduct team-building sessions.
- Human resource professionals who teach their managers how to use this tool.

### Processing the Activity:

- Distribute questionnaire. Ask participants to focus on their own team as they put a check in the appropriate column.
- Put people in pairs or small groups so they can discuss their responses.
- Identify *no* answers on which there is consensus.
- Discuss results and perceptions among the whole group.
- Make two lists on the easel and flip chart. One label is *Greatest Strengths*. The other is *Need to Improve*. Get responses from the group about which items go where.
- Discuss where the biggest weaknesses lie and what you want to do about them.

### Questions for Discussion:

- What are your/the team's greatest strengths? Areas ripe for improvement?
- What happens if we/you do nothing?
- If we/you decided to select one area for improvement right now, which one would have the largest impact on our performance?
- What would you do differently the next time you give feedback to diverse employees?

### Caveats and Considerations:

- If you have many different cultures represented, some people who are less acculturated to the mainstream may have a hard time speaking up about the group's weaknesses.
- Put people in small groups with those they trust and with whom they feel comfortable. That will produce the most involvement and best data.
- Respect people's reluctance. Work with them quietly and slowly to build trust. Over time, you will get more participation and openness.
- Get the cooperation of informal group leaders and you will increase chances of getting the data and participation you want.

# Understanding How Cultural Lenses
# Impact Teamsmanship

In order to understand how culture shapes these four values, and the impact of these value differences on the effectiveness of your team, look at the following continua. For each, mark an X at the point that appropriately expresses your values as seen through demonstrated behavior. Once you have marked all four, connect the Xs to get a values profile.

**1.** ..............................................................................................................................................

**Value on
harmony**
                                                                                              **Value on
                                                                                           surfacing
                                                                                    and resolving
                                                                                       differences**

**2.** ..............................................................................................................................................

**Status based
on family or
connections**
                                                                                      **Status based on
                                                                                              merit or
                                                                                        achievement**

**3.** ..............................................................................................................................................

**Emphasis on
the group**
                                                                                          **Emphasis on
                                                                                         the individual**

**4.** ..............................................................................................................................................

**External locus
of control**
                                                                                         **Internal locus
                                                                                            of control**

## Suggestions for Using *Understanding How Cultural Lenses Impact Teamsmanship*

### Objectives:

- Illustrate the impact that culture has on values.
- Show graphically how culture and values impact team dynamics.
- Gain awareness about similarities and differences between self and team members in four key areas that influence team performance.

### Intended Audience:

- Any work team facilitated by a manager, an HR professional, or an internal or external consultant or trainer.

### Processing the Activity:

- Distribute the learning activity and a different color of marker or pen to each participant.
- Discuss four values and the opposite ends of the continuum regarding each. Then ask participants to put an *X* at the spot that most accurately reflects their values.
- Ask participants to draw a values profile by connecting dots. Put their name on the paper and, with masking tape, put their profile on the wall.
- Ask participants to get up, walk around the room, and see the different profiles. When finished, they come back to their seats.

### Questions for Discussion:

- What surprised you, or what did you notice about yourself when marking your own responses?
- When you walked around and saw other team members' profiles, what struck you?
- What seem to be the areas of greatest similarity?
- Where do we seem to have the most difference?
- What can we do to minimize the conflict from differences?
- How can we make the differences work for us? Make us stronger?

### Caveats and Considerations:

- If you have some people who seem reticent, process the discussion in small groups first.

# Cross-Cultural Team-Building Scale

Directions: All human beings have values preferences that significantly impact work group cohesion. To see your values profile, mark an *X* along the continuum for each item and then connect the *X*s. The benefit of this exercise to your team is that you will all see where the similarities and differences are. From there, the next step is to discuss how you make your individual differences a collective advantage.

| | | |
|---|---|---|
| Value change | ................................................ | Value tradition |
| Specificity in communicating | ................................................ | Vagueness in communicating |
| Analytical, linear problem solving | ................................................ | Intuitive, lateral problem solving |
| Emphasis on individual performance | ................................................ | Emphasis on group performance |
| Communication primarily verbal | ................................................ | Communication primarily nonverbal |
| Emphasis on task and product | ................................................ | Emphasis on relationship and process |
| Surface different views | ................................................ | Harmony |
| More horizontal organization | ................................................ | More vertical organization |
| Informal tone | ................................................ | Formal tone |
| Competition | ................................................ | Collaboration |
| Rigid adherence to time | ................................................ | Flexible adherence to time |

## Suggestions for Using the *Cross-Cultural Team-Building Scale*

**Objectives:**

* Understand how different values impact work-group cohesion.
* Identify cultural differences that influence team functioning.

**Intended Audience:**

* Members of any functional work team.
* Any manager, facilitator, internal/external consultant, HR professional, or trainer charged with the task of creating a cohesive team.

**Processing the Activity:**

* Discuss and define each of the items on the continuum.
* Ask team members to mark an *X* where they see their own values. Then connect the dots to see the values profile.
* Divide members into small groups. Ask them to compare their individual profiles.
* Come back to the whole group for discussion.

**Questions for Discussion:**

* What values similarities and differences were most notable among group members?
* What surprises, if any, did you find in the responses of any of your team members?
* When you look more closely at the values differences, what impact do they or might they have on our team?
* How can we make those differences work in our favor?

**Caveats and Considerations:**

* Refer back to the worksheet in this chapter called *Understanding How Cultural Lenses Impact Teamsmanship* (p.109) The suggestions for processing that activity may be appropriate for the *Cross-Cultural Team-Building Scale* as well.
* After people fill out the scale, compare the various profiles and talk about the implications of the differences. Ask the group for their suggestions on how to use this information productively while honoring the various norms. Depending on the size of the team, you might break people into small groups, getting a good cross-cultural mix in each. But asking the group to come up with some suggestions for how to get maximum input, involvement, harmony, and support while respecting values differences will be helpful and enlightening. The responses will give you pertinent information, while the process will help you create a team where esteem and belonging needs are met.

# Increasing Esteem and Belonging
# on Your Team

Directions: In the space below, write down your suggestions for increasing esteem and belonging of all team members.

| Suggestions for Increasing Esteem and Belonging | How to Do It |
|---|---|
| 1. Identify and build on shared values | |
| 2. Get commitment to the group's goals and objectives | |
| 3. Reward excellence | |
| 4. Demonstrate an appreciation for each person and each culture's uniqueness | |
| 5. Acknowledge cultural conflicts | |
| 6. Become more culturally sensitive | |
| 7. Engage in activity team building | |
| 8. Acknowledge cultural differences | |

# Suggestions for Using *Increasing Esteem and Belonging on Your Team*

## Objectives:

- Explore ways to have all team members feel more valued and included.
- Gain commitment of all team members toward this goal.
- Create realization that all team members are responsible for the climate or atmosphere on a team.

## Intended Audience:

- Members of any functional work team.
- Any manager, facilitator, internal/external consultant, HR professional, or trainer charged with the task of creating a more cohesive, high-performing team.

## Processing the Activity:

- The manager, facilitator, or trainer discusses the importance of members' getting esteem and belonging needs met in order to have a highly productive unit.
- Discuss each of the eight items on the worksheet and what they contribute to increased esteem and belonging needs, and their collective impact on performance.
- Then divide the group into small groups of approximately four to seven participants in each, depending on the number of people.
- Give groups the task of coming up with suggestions for each of the eight areas. How many each group is responsible for depends on the number of groups you have.
- Each group will write their ideas on chart paper so the suggestions can eventually be typed up and distributed.
- When finished brainstorming ideas, each group will report their suggestions to the whole group. That will provide an opportunity to add suggestions, answer questions, or modify any comments.

## Questions for Discussion:

- Where can we pat ourselves on the back for already creating a healthy climate and helping employees get esteem and belonging needs met?
- Were some of the eight items harder to come up with suggestions for than others? If so, which ones?
- How do we (you) hold one another accountable so these suggestions become our norm?
- Which ones might make the most and best difference in our (your) functioning?
- What is the one thing I (you/each of us) will begin doing tommorow to make this happen?

# Goal Clarification Sheet

A team's mission determines its goals and direction. A team's reason for being is an essential step in developing team unity and is effective to the degree that the mission is both clear and agreed on. As a beginning step in goal clarification, define your team's mission as you perceive it.

**Goal Clarification**

My team's mission is:

_____

_____

_____

What goals logically follow from this mission?

_____

_____

**Role Clarification**

To implement these goals, my role/responsibilities are:

_____        _____

_____        _____

_____        _____

Other member's roles and responsibilities are:

| **Name** | **Role** |
|---|---|
| _____ | _____ |
| _____ | _____ |
| _____ | _____ |

To carry out my responsibility, I need from you:

| **Name** | **Need to Get** | **Need to Give** |
|---|---|---|
| _____ | _____ | _____ |
| _____ | _____ | _____ |
| _____ | _____ | _____ |

# Suggestions for Using the *Goal Clarification Sheet*

**Objectives:**

- Articulate and define the team's mission.
- Determine what goals follow from this mission.
- Clarify roles and responsibilities in order to accomplish these goals.

**Intended Audience:**

- Members of any functional work team.
- Any manager, facilitator, internal or external consultant, HR professional, or trainer who is helping the team define its purpose and clarify who does what.

**Processing the Activity:**

- Ask each team member to fill out the mission statement first. Suggest looking at an abstract rather than a concrete statement of purpose.
- Record each team member's statement on an easel in front of the group.
- Look for points of agreement and build on those. Reword till all agree with the statement.
- Then ask each person to list the top three objectives that logically follow from that mission statement.
- Go around the group and again, on an easel, list all suggestions. Indicate repeated suggestions with checks in a different color marker from that with which you are writing.
- Discuss all suggestions and through group discussion and reference back to mission statement, decide on the top three.
- Based on that outcome, have each person write down his or her responsibilities and those of other team members as the person sees them.
- Then in rotating one-on-one rounds that last about 15 minutes each, have people negotiate their roles and expectations with one another.

**Questions for Discussion:**

- Are there any semantic or language issues that are getting in the way of defining our mission? If so, how can we say things so all people support the statement?
- Of all the goals listed, which will help us get closest to accomplishing our mission?
- Is there any role or responsibility that is still not clear after negotiations?

**Caveats and Considerations:**

- This is a lengthy process. Rarely do groups have the luxury to do it all at once. But you can break it up into parts that break naturally. The mission statement definition may take one or two sessions. Defining goals can take one, and defining roles and responsibilities another. If you do this at a team-building retreat rather than on work time, it can be done in one session.
- Team members need to be acculturated to fully participate in this process.

# Team-Building Response Sheet
# (A Tool to Increase Cohesion
# through Feedback)

This series of open-ended statements is intended to help you discover and clarify your reactions, opinions, and thoughts about your job and organization. You will have a chance to share and learn from other group members' responses. Directions are as follows: (1) Take turns initiating the discussion, (2) complete responses orally, and (3) respond to statements in any order you choose.

1.  Basically, my job is . . .

2.  Usually, I am the kind of person who . . .

3.  When things aren't going well, I . . .

4.  When I'm confused or not sure what to do, I . . .

5.  On the job, I'm best at . . .

6.  One place where I could use some improvement is . . .

7.  The best boss I ever had . . .

8.  The strength of this group lies in . . .

9.  One thing this group could do differently to be more of a team is . . .

10. A work group is positive and constructive for me when . . .

11. I am most involved and excited about my job when . . .

12. When I am approaching a deadline, I . . .

13. As a member of a team, I . . .

14. I prefer to work with people who . . .

15. I can help my team by . . .

# Suggestions for Using the *Team-Building Response Sheet*

### Objectives:

- Clarify and discover each team member's reactions, opinions, and thoughts about the team, job, and organization.
- Learn more about other team members' reactions, opinions, and thoughts.
- Build trust and openness on the team.

### Intended Audience:

- Members of any functional work team.
- Any facilitator, manager, consultant, or HR professional leading a team through trust-building or feedback activities.

### Processing the Activity:

- State purpose of activity. Tell participants not to write answers down. Just discuss responses orally.
- Divide into pairs or small groups. Have people discuss responses.
- Discuss some responses in whole group afterward.

### Questions for Discussion:

- What information or responses were the most surprising or interesting to you?
- Which were easiest for you to answer? Which were most difficult?
- What's the biggest insight or learning you got about yourself? Your team members?
- What should we do with this learning?

### Caveats and Considerations:

- The way you divide people (pairs or larger groups) and whether or not you ask them to group with those they know best or least has to do with trust level and your objective.
- Even with those who think they know each other best, there will be new information and surprises.
- Pairs are best when trying to provide safety and security; bigger groups are better when trying to show breadth of differences and perspectives.

# Norms/Values Worksheet

1. Pass a sheet of paper out to each team member.

2. Ask participants to think about values or norms they currently see at work that are different from those found in their culture of birth. Once they identify several, have them make two lists as indicated below, with those values they like in one column and those that are difficult to deal with in the other.

3. The manager or facilitator collects the information from each person and then has someone read the data aloud while the manager/facilitator charts the information on the chart paper or on an overhead. If you prefer to have each team member involved in reading the data aloud, shuffle the lists, then redistribute them and have each person read the data aloud from a colleague's list.

4. Once the data are posted, you can ask the group to identify benefits of the values that are hard for people to deal with. Use the expertise of group members who have found a way to deal with different cultural values successfully. End with concrete suggestions for how to handle the ones that may get in the way. If this is facilitated well, it can be enormously helpful. (We will give you information about effective facilitation in Chapter 5.)

| Norms/Values<br>I Like and Enjoy | Norms/Values that Are<br>Difficult for Me |
|---|---|
| Make people and relationships a high priority (example) | Lack of time consciousness and directness (example) |

# Suggestions for Using the *Norms/Values Worksheet*

**Objectives:**

- Identify any cross-cultural values and norms that may be difficult for individual team members to deal with.
- Identify ways to more effectively deal with those values and norms that are a problem.

**Intended Audience:**

- Members of any functional work team.
- Any facilitator, trainer, manager, internal or external consultant, or HR professional who will process the activity.

**Processing the Activity:**

- Pass the worksheet to each team member.
- Ask them to think about values or norms different from theirs.
- In one column list those they like and enjoy; in the other, list those that are difficult for them.
- Collect the information from everyone and have one member read all answers aloud. The facilitator charts them.
- Get suggestions from group members about how to deal effectively with those that may be hard for some while not so hard for others.

**Questions for Discussion:**

- What ways have some of you found to deal with these norms that no longer make them a problem?

**Caveats and Considerations:**

- Collecting everyone's paper and having the data remain anonymous as one person reads all the information will maximize the learning and get beyond cultural discomfort.
- You can collect and redistribute papers so no one has to be accountable for reading his or her own.

# Window on the Team

| What's going well on this team? | What are areas of concern? |
|---|---|
| | |
| **What skills would help you be a better team member?** | **What kind of support helps you be a more productive team member?** |
| | |

# Suggestions for Using *Window on the Team*

**Objectives:**

- Stimulate individual thought and discussion that will lead to usable information for the whole team.
- Gain perspective and information about the team.

**Intended Audience:**

- All members of any functional work team.
- Managers, facilitators, consultants, or HR professionals who can facilitate the activity.

**Processing the Activity:**

- Ask participants to fill out information in all four quadrants.
- Pair up to discuss.
- Get information in top two quadrants from everyone and chart it on an easel and flip chart.

**Questions for Discussion:**

- What does this tell you about our (your) team?
- What kinds of support would help you be a better team member?
- What do the data suggest you (we) used to do to be stronger?

**Caveats and Considerations:**

- In a small group (six or seven people) you can share data from everyone.
- You can change the questions or areas of focus to suit any need you have at a given time.

# Team Development Survey

Please respond to items 1 through 6 by circling the appropriate answer. There is no right answer, only your answer, honestly given, based on your perception. Data will be reported collectively so the anonymity of each person is assured.

1. I am clear about our team's goals and priorities.

| 1 | 2 | 3 | 4 | 5 |
|---|---|---|---|---|
| Rarely | | Sometimes | | Almost always |

2. I am influential in setting priorities and making decisions.

| 1 | 2 | 3 | 4 | 5 |
|---|---|---|---|---|
| Rarely | | Sometimes | | Almost always |

3. As a team, we are effective in dealing with our differences.

| 1 | 2 | 3 | 4 | 5 |
|---|---|---|---|---|
| Rarely | | Sometimes | | Almost always |

4. On this team, it is safe to honestly express my values and ideas.

| 1 | 2 | 3 | 4 | 5 |
|---|---|---|---|---|
| Rarely | | Sometimes | | Almost always |

5. We have clear roles and responsibilities.

| 1 | 2 | 3 | 4 | 5 |
|---|---|---|---|---|
| Rarely | | Sometimes | | Almost always |

6. The goals of this team and this organization are meaningful to me.

| 1 | 2 | 3 | 4 | 5 |
|---|---|---|---|---|
| Rarely | | Sometimes | | Almost always |

Please respond to the following questions by writing down your candid responses on the lines below.

1.  The strengths of this team are

_____

_____

2.  In order for this team to be more effective, it needs to

_____

_____

3.  What I expect from this day, or what would be most helpful to me is

_____

_____

# Suggestions for Using the *Team Development Survey*

## Objectives:

- Give the team feedback about itself in a number of different areas.
- Gain information objectively and subjectively through numerical responses and open-ended statements.

## Intended Audience:

- Members of any functional work team.
- Any facilitator, manager, consultant, or HR professional leading a team through trust-building or feedback activities.

## Processing the Activity:

- Ask team members to fill their responses out; you collect the worksheets.
- The facilitator compiles data and feeds the compiled data back to the group.

## Questions for Discussion:

- What does this information tell you (us) about what the team is doing well and what it is not?
- How do you account for the range in numbers (from a low score of 2 to a high score of 5, for example)?
- How do the objective data fit with your open-ended responses?
- Based on this information, what issues does the team need to address?

## Caveats and Considerations:

- You can collect this information ahead of the session and use it to plan the agenda of an initial team-building session. It legitimizes the direction you take with a group because the content comes straight out of their information. But you can also use this right at the session and tabulate the data on the spot and use the information to generate discussion on various dimensions of team effectiveness.

# Group Experience Rating Form

Instructions: Rate the problem-solving performance of your group by responding to the questions below. Indicate for each question the rating (1–5) that most nearly describes your observation of the group experience. Simply circle the appropriate number. The scale is as follows:

| 1 | 2 | 3 | 4 | 5 |
|---|---|---|---|---|
| Seldom | | | | Always |

**Members in this Group**

| | | | | | | |
|---|---|---|---|---|---|---|
| 1. | Take time to find out what the problem really is. | 1 | 2 | 3 | 4 | 5 |
| 2. | Listen and try to understand my viewpoint. | 1 | 2 | 3 | 4 | 5 |
| 3. | Understand the feelings I may be experiencing. | 1 | 2 | 3 | 4 | 5 |
| 4. | Help me to clarify my thinking. | 1 | 2 | 3 | 4 | 5 |
| 5. | Repeat and clarify what I have said before making their own statement. | 1 | 2 | 3 | 4 | 5 |
| 6. | Ask clarifying, insightful questions. | 1 | 2 | 3 | 4 | 5 |
| 7. | Share their feelings about the team's strengths and weaknesses. | 1 | 2 | 3 | 4 | 5 |
| 8. | Offer loyalty, support, and encouragement to me. | 1 | 2 | 3 | 4 | 5 |
| 9. | Give me a chance to talk and encourage my contributions. | 1 | 2 | 3 | 4 | 5 |
| 10. | Help me explore alternatives without pushing their own solutions. | 1 | 2 | 3 | 4 | 5 |
| 11. | Set out to find the facts. | 1 | 2 | 3 | 4 | 5 |
| 12. | Take time to set goals and objectives. | 1 | 2 | 3 | 4 | 5 |
| 13. | Take time to evaluate how we are doing individually and collectively. | 1 | 2 | 3 | 4 | 5 |
| 14. | Put talk and decisions into action. | 1 | 2 | 3 | 4 | 5 |
| 15. | Seek and accept help from others. | 1 | 2 | 3 | 4 | 5 |
| 16. | Provide different functions to the team at different times (e.g., leader, clarifier, summarizer, etc.). | 1 | 2 | 3 | 4 | 5 |
| 17. | Say clearly, but sensitively, what they need or expect from me and others. | 1 | 2 | 3 | 4 | 5 |
| 18. | Face disagreements and seek to understand them. | 1 | 2 | 3 | 4 | 5 |
| 19. | Seem to care about me and other team members and whether or not we accomplish our best goals. | 1 | 2 | 3 | 4 | 5 |
| 20. | Give honest, nonjudgmental feedback. | 1 | 2 | 3 | 4 | 5 |

# Suggestions for Using the *Group Experience Rating Form*

### Objectives:

- Assess the function and behaviors of the team.
- See which behaviors add to team effectiveness and which detract.
- Get a sense of the various perspectives team members hold.

### Intended Audience:

- Members of any functional work team.
- Any facilitator, manager, consultant, or HR professional leading a team through trust-building or feedback activities.

### Processing the Activity:

- Ask each team member to rate the team by responding to the 20 items.
- Discuss responses in pairs or small groups first, then in large groups.
- Based on responses, determine an area to work on.

### Questions for Discussion:

- What are the areas of greatest strength? Greatest weakness?
- What does this rating form suggest this team needs to do differently?
- Focusing on what item will help this team the most?

### Caveats and Considerations:

- If 20 items feel like too many, divide items in half or quarters. Start smaller and eventually work through all 20 items.

# How Much of a Relationship Nurturer Are You?

_____ I spend time with every staff member each week.

_____ I make it a point to circulate through the areas of my department every day.

_____ Employees often come to see me.

_____ I often eat lunch or take breaks with my employees.

_____ I know a little about the personal lives of each of my staff people.

_____ I can usually tell when someone needs to talk.

_____ Employees seem relaxed and comfortable around me.

_____ I sometimes talk about non-work-related topics with my staff members.

_____ I let my staff know I appreciate them.

_____ I greet each employee every day.

_____ I help staff through the rough times.

# Meeting Climate Survey

Directions: Identify a group with whom you have regular meetings, either as a leader or a participant. Think back to the last six meetings you have had with this group. Then respond to the questions below with the most appropriate answer. To make this tool even more useful, pass it out at one of your meetings when your goal is to assess how you are doing as a group and how effective your meetings are. Once your participants have responded, you can see where your climate is thriving and where it also might be sagging.

| Questions | Almost Always | Sometimes | Almost Never |
|---|---|---|---|
| 1. The environment is easy and comfortable, even when discussing thorny issues. | _____ | _____ | _____ |
| 2. Enthusiasm and participation at meetings is high. | _____ | _____ | _____ |
| 3. New, unconventional ideas are suggested. | _____ | _____ | _____ |
| 4. Different points of view on any issue are welcome and encouraged. | _____ | _____ | _____ |
| 5. Many ideas are cultivated; none are ridiculed. | _____ | _____ | _____ |
| 6. People speak their minds. | _____ | _____ | _____ |
| 7. It is no secret where everyone stands on the issues that come up. | _____ | _____ | _____ |
| 8. There is respect for principles of others, however unpopular the view. | _____ | _____ | _____ |
| 9. Clarifying, and sometimes challenging, questions are asked in warm, unhostile tones. | _____ | _____ | _____ |
| 10. Positions change as a result of discussions on the issues. | _____ | _____ | _____ |
| 11. Feedback is given sensitively and constructively. | _____ | _____ | _____ |
| 12. Relevant and appropriate self-disclosure on any issue occurs. | _____ | _____ | _____ |
| 13. Group members build on the ideas of others, and they volunteer to help when help is warranted. | _____ | _____ | _____ |
| 14. There is a "can do" attitude. | _____ | _____ | _____ |
| 15. Group members follow through on their responsibilities. | _____ | _____ | _____ |

# Meeting Climate Survey *(concluded)*

Directions for scoring: Record the appropriate point count for each of you answers.
- Each "Almost always" answer is 3 points.
- Each "Sometimes" answer is 2 points.
- Each "Almost never" answer is 1 point.

1. _____    9. _____

2. _____    10. _____

3. _____    11. _____

4. _____    12. _____

5. _____    13. _____

6. _____    14. _____

7. _____    15. _____

8. _____    Total: _____

The closer your point count is to 45, the more open your climate is.

| **Trust and openness:** | **numbers 1, 7, 10** |
|---|---|
| Morale: | numbers 2, 11, 14 |
| Responsibility: | numbers 3, 6, 15 |
| Support: | numbers 4, 9, 13 |
| Freedom: | numbers 5, 8, 12 |

**Trust and openness:** The amount of safety and security one feels in giving an honest opinion and trusting these views will be valued and respected; this also looks at how open participants are to new ideas.

**Morale:** The feelings of confidence in the group's ability to accomplish its goals and get the job done in the face of the predictable roadblocks. There is also the sense that differences will be dealt with in sensitive and productive ways.

**Responsibility:** The willingness of participants to follow through on their tasks and be held accountable; also the willingness to take initiative in putting forth ideas and voicing reactions to any ideas suggested.

**Support:** Both emotional and task support are involved. The first shows appreciation for the person who sticks his neck out to say something unpopular. The latter involves taking the initiative without being asked.

**Freedom:** A real tolerance for differences without fear of recrimination or ostracism; the feeling that you can be honest about ideas or reactions and it won't cost you in your relationships or opportunities.

The questionnaire will evaluate your group in these five areas. The information you get will show you how open and trusting your climate is. Once you get the diagnosis from the group, you can then determine appropriate courses of action.

# Suggestions for Using the *Meeting Climate Survey*

**Objectives:**

- Get a sense of the climate in which your meetings are conducted.
- Evaluate meetings in five areas: trust and openness, morale, responsibility, support, and freedom.

**Intended Audience:**

- Managers seeking feedback from the work group on the climate at meetings.
- Any facilitator, internal or external consultant, HR professional, or trainer helping managers understand the importance of an open climate in creating a productive meeting environment.
- Trainers, facilitators, consultants, and HR professionals who want to assess the climate they create at their workshops and seminars.

**Processing the Activity:**

- Ask participants to think of their last six meetings with one particular group and then respond to the questions.
- Have participants score the questionnaire.
- Discuss each of the five concepts being measured and discuss their connection to an inviting climate.
- Have people break up into small groups and discuss their own responses, paying particular attention to one-point answers. If participants have no one-point answers, suggest they look at two-point answers.
- Have participants do an item analysis to determine their meeting climate weaknesses.

**Questions for Discussion:**

- Is there any pattern to your one- or two-point answers?
- If so, what is it?
- What does this survey suggest you need to do differently to improve your meeting climate?

**Caveats and Considerations:**

- This questionnaire can be facilitated by a manager wanting a work group to evaluate their own meetings, but it can also be used as a training tool for managers focusing on their meetings and how to improve them.

# Group Process Questionnaire

Answer the following questions by putting a check in either the Yes or No column. If your answer is yes, estimate the percentage of your meetings where you use what you've checked off and enter that percentage in the frequency column. For example, if you use the random count method about two thirds of the time, put 65%. If you use pairs in every meeting, your response might be 100%.

| Use of Small Groups | Yes | No | Frequency |
|---|---|---|---|
| **Method of Configuring the Group** | | | |
| Random count | | | |
| Job alike | | | |
| Mixed groups | | | |
| Self-selection | | | |
| **Numbers of People in the Group** | | | |
| Pairs (can be someone you trust, or maybe just someone you are sitting next to) | | | |
| Triads (you can count off randomly or ask participants to find two people they feel comfortable with) | | | |
| Any number of people but it depends on purpose, number of participants and other factors; 7 to 9 are ideal for problem solving while groups of 4 or 5 are excellent for processing information and seeking input on various issues | | | |

# Group Process Questionnaire (*concluded*)

| Use of Small Groups | Yes | No | Frequency |
|---|---|---|---|
| **Publishing Data** | | | |
| Collect data at central point and use flip chart | | | |
| Collect data on overhead or blackboard at central point | | | |
| Have various subgroups; generate data, record on board or flip chart, then report | | | |
| Synthesize data at central point after each group has recorded and reported its data | | | |
| **Input-Seeking Techniques** | | | |
| Open-ended statements given from overhead, easel, or on a handout (e.g., The best thing about this policy is . . .) | | | |
| Paper-and-pencil questionnaires | | | |
| Index cards (3 × 5 or 5 × 8) as a tool for writing questions/concerns, information, or organizing thoughts | | | |

# Suggestions for Using the *Group Process Questionnaire*

**Objectives:**

- Determine how interactive the processes are at your meetings.

**Intended Audience:**

- Managers who want to evaluate their own meetings.
- Trainers, facilitators, consultants, and HR professionals who want to get a sense of their own group process in meetings or the training sessions they design.

**Processing the Activity:**

- Have participants fill out the questionnaires.
- In small groups, discuss the results and implications.
- After you've looked at the data, indicate what changes need to be made in order to more effectively use group process.

**Questions for Discussion:**

- Which techniques and methods do you use the most?
- Are there some you rarely use that might make your meetings/sessions more interactive?
- What one would you be willing to try at your very next meeting or seminar?

**Caveats and Considerations:**

- Use of small groups where trust is high is critical to helping newcomers acculturate to American business norms.

# The Hows and Whys of Warm-Ups

**Purpose**

- Focus participants on task or topic

- Get initial, immediate involvement of participants

**Methods (Depends on size of group, time available, and amount of involvement required)**

- Question to think about
  *(Think of the most successful work unit . . . .)*

- Polling the group
  *(How many of you have . . . .)*

- Random responses from group
  *(What are some examples of . . . .)*

- Individual oral response
  *(Good management is . . . .)*

- Share/interview in pairs
  *(Assorted topics.)*

**Forms**

- Open-ended statements
  *(My biggest concern about _____ is . . . .)*

- Respond to question
  *(What behaviors do you see in good managers?)*

- Topics for sharing/interviewing
  *(High/low points of year, best/worst aspects of this plan/project, what I want to achieve/avoid in doing this project.)*

- Analyze incident from experience
  *(Think of your most successful/unsuccessful meeting.)*

- Goal setting
  *(Expectations, what I want to get, what is the best/worst that could come from this session?)*

**Tips for Warm-Ups**

- Remember to keep warm-up relevant and quick

- Only chart information if it will be used

# Sample Agenda

**Purpose:** To begin the process of improving interdepartmental communication.

**Objectives:** To identify the strengths and weaknesses of the interdepartmental communication process as it currently exists.

**Process:**
**Warm-Up:** Each participant in the meeting responds to the following open-ended statements while the facilitator charts all responses on the flip chart at the front of the room.

1. **The best thing about our interdepartmental communication is**

_____

2. **The most frustrating thing about it is**

_____

After the facilitator records all the responses to these two questions on a flip chart, lead a group discussion about their responses to the data. Center the responses around three areas: (1) reactions, (2) surprises, and (3) insights. It may be helpful to write those three words on the flip chart in order to focus the discussion. Use the group's comments as a lead to get into the next part of the agenda, which is the _Personal Focus Activity_. While this worksheet offers a sample of a data gathering technique, you can change the content to make it relevant for you.

# Personal Focus Activity
## (Interdepartmental Communication Process)

| | My Department | Other Department |
|---|---|---|
| **Procedures that Get in the Way** | | |
| **Procedures that Help** | | |

# Agenda Planning Worksheet

Purpose:




Objectives:






Process:
  Warm-up:

  Activity:

  Grouping:

  Leadership:

  Closure/next steps:


Logistics:
  Place:

  Time:


Preplanning:
  Publicity:

  Materials:

  Refreshments:

# Suggestions for Using the *Agenda Planning Worksheet*

**Objectives:**

- Provide a structure to design effective meetings.

**Intended Audience:**

- Any person who plans meetings, training sessions, workshops, or seminars.

**Processing the Activity:**

- Offer this as a suggested structure that people can use over and over again.

**Questions for Discussion:**

- Are there any pieces of the agenda planning guide that are unclear?
- What questions do you have or what clarifications do you need?

**Caveats and Considerations:**

- Help people see the application. Sometimes only managers think this applies, but task forces and ad hoc committees can also use this information.

# How Effective a Facilitator Are You?

Directions: Rate yourself from 1 to 5 on the following facilitator skills. The closer you are to a *5,* the more skilled you are at facilitation.

| Facilitator Behavior | 1 | 2 | 3 | 4 | 5 |
|---|---|---|---|---|---|
| 1.  Remains neutral | | | | | |
| 2.  Does not judge or contribute ideas | | | | | |
| 3.  Keeps the group focused on common task | | | | | |
| 4.  Asks clarifying, helpful questions that suggest alternatives | | | | | |
| 5.  Creates a climate free of attack or criticism | | | | | |
| 6.  Encourages and structures participation | | | | | |
| 7.  Helps the group find win/ win solutions | | | | | |

## Suggestions for Using *How Effective a Facilitator Are You?*

### Objectives:

- Evaluate facilitation skills.
- Determine areas for growth.

### Intended Audience:

- Managers facilitating meetings.
- HR professionals, facilitators, consultants, and trainers who lead meetings, problem-solving sessions, or workshops where their neutrality is essential.

### Processing the Activity:

- Distribute the questionnaire and ask participants to focus on a meeting or seminar they recently led.
- With that session in mind, ask participants to rate themselves on a 1 to 5 scale, 5 being the best.
- Have participants then pair up (or use small groups) and discuss their evaluations.
- Ask them to focus on what this questionnaire suggests their facilitation strengths and weaknesses are and what they need to do differently.

### Questions for Discussion:

- How did you feel while you were filling this out?
- What good news did you discover about your facilitation skills?
- What do you think those who attend your workshops and meetings would say about your skills?
- What do the data suggest you need to do differently in order to improve your skills?
- What suggestions can you give one another (in pairs or small groups) that will be helpful to you?

### Caveats and Considerations:

- Small groups increase safety and security when having people discuss their insights and then get feedback.
- Putting two sets of pairs together for the last discussion questions may increase the number of ideas offered.

# The Impact of Cultural Norms on Meetings

| Cultural Norms | Impact on Meetings | What to Do |
|---|---|---|
| **Respect for authority** | This norm leads to an unwillingness to challenge ideas from people of a certain age or title; may inhibit solutions to problem solving and can lead to a more formal climate. | State expectations emphasizing the need for participation because it will benefit the company. Loyalty is also a norm that you can use here. Show respect to the group's informal leader because of age, knowledge, title, and overall influence. Solicit this person's help and give leaders the same esteem groups do. |
| **Emphasis on group over individual** | This may lead some managers to assume people are unmotivated or lazy because they keep pace with the team rather than seek individual glory or promotion. | The group is your best cultural ally. Use it! Stress teamwork, harmony, and collaboration. Structure group tasks and focus on group accomplishment. |
| **Fear of shame and loss of face** | Because people are afraid to lose face or make mistakes, there might be less willingness to take risks or share unconventional ideas. | Talk about the importance of taking intelligent risks and reinforce this even when the group makes mistakes. Avoid finger pointing or blaming. Make the group motto be "We're all in this together." Encourage their risk taking and reward their efforts. |
| **More contextual, less direct communication** | It is harder in less direct cultures to figure out what is really on someone's mind. This can result in miscommunication, both in and out of meetings. | Develop a good, trusting relationship over time. It will take time to understand the subtle nuance as well as to get people to open up. You may never get the straight talk the way Americans give it. But you can pay attention to the subtle nonverbal cues. With trust and a good relationship you'll develop understanding over time. |

# The Impact of Cultural Norms on Meetings *(concluded)*

| Cultural Norms | Impact on Meetings | What to Do |
|---|---|---|
| **Value placed on harmony and collaboration** | This norm mostly works to your advantage in having people create a positive working environment. The downside may be an unwillingness to discuss painful truths for the sake of harmony, even though it may be necessary. | Use the question asking skills presented in the chapter on interviewing. In sensitive ways and an unthreatening tone, seek information that may be necessary, and do so through the informal system. Remember to use the group. That provides safety and minimizes the sting. |
| **Family as the first priority** | There are times when people, particularly from Mexico and Central America, may need to leave to take care of family priorities. They may miss meetings, and more important, the assignments that result from them. Deadlines may not be met. | Work with people to find the middle ground. No one wants to be insensitive in times of family emergency. There are always trade-offs. Explain them. The group may pick up a person's slack for a short time. If a pattern develops that permanently inhibits work flow, some choices will have to be made. |
| **Time consciousness: some cultures hold tighter time lines than the dominant culture, some looser** | The rules need to be the same for everyone or there will be disgruntlement. Be careful not to interpret some laissez-faire behavior regarding time as indications of laziness or lack of caring. | Make clear what the meeting norms and expectations are. Once you decide how strict or loose you are going to be regarding time lines, reinforce your "rules." Position being on time as showing respect to other members of the group. |
| **Problem solving that is less linear and analytical** | You sometimes may feel like you aren't getting anywhere, because again, American directness likes to go straight for the solution. But lateral, intuitive thinking adds its own unique contribution to the process. | Learn to value and utilize different ways of thinking. This difference is truly one of the biggest gifts from diversity. Don't immediately discount nonlinear, nonlogical methods. |
| **Goal setting and planning influenced by fatalism** | The external locus of control mentality mentioned earlier may create the appearance in some cultures that people are less driven or motivated. Again, it's probably cultural. Belief in God's will is a powerful shaper. | Help your work group experience the direct connection between the responsibility they accept and the results they get. This will be a whole new way of viewing the world for some people whose life experience has not shown them that they have much influence over their own world. Patience, respect, and positive reinforcement will help. |

# Meeting Planning Checklist

Use this checklist in planning your next meeting, then again as an evaluation after the meeting. Target weaker areas for improvement in subsequent meetings. You will find that more effective meetings mean not only greater productivity but more enthusiastic followership, both keys to your success as a leader.

### Preplanning

_____ Have facilities and equipment reserved, set up, and functional.

_____ Suit room size and seating arrangements to group size and activity.

_____ Have materials prepared and distributed when necessary.

_____ Make accomodations for refreshments and offer alternatives (e.g., tea, decaf, juice, etc.).

_____ Make sure location is accessible.

### Clarifying Purpose and Objectives

_____ Have clear outcome in mind for each meeting.

_____ Prepare participants by giving clear expectations of the purpose of the meeting.

_____ Realistically match desired objectives to available time.

### Agenda Planning

_____ Use a relevant warm-up that is quick, purposeful, and focusing.

_____ Include a variety of activities (e.g., writing, listening, discussing).

_____ Structure activities which require everyone to participate.

_____ Make sure data collected are visible to all (e.g., on blackboard, flip chart, etc.).

_____ Summarize the accomplishments of the meeting and indicate next steps.

### Getting Participation

_____ Use small groups for discussing and sharing information to increase input and output.

_____ Use different groupings appropriately (e.g., random, like-job, work units, etc.).

_____ Break down large tasks into small steps with progress checks throughout.

_____ Encourage passive participants to join in activities.

_____ Pay attention to the needs of the participants.

### Evaluation and Closure

_____ Clearly define responsibilities resulting from the meeting.

_____ Set the time and place for progress checks.

_____ Get feedback from participants about the meeting (oral or written).

_____ Do a personal analysis of the meeting, focusing on accomplishment and participation.

# Suggestions for Using the *Meeting Planning Checklist*

**Objectives:**

- Provide a meeting evaluation tool.

**Intended Audience:**

- Managers or executives who plan and lead meetings.
- Trainers, consultants, or HR professionals who plan training seminars, workshops, or meetings.

**Processing the Activity:**

- Think about the last meeting/training seminar/workshop you planned.
- With that session in mind, use the *Meeting Planning Checklist* as an evaluation tool.
- Put people in pairs to discuss their evaluations.
- Note the items where you were able to put checks. More important, note the items where you had none.

**Questions for Discussion:**

- What does this tell you that you did well at your last meeting? What could you have done better?
- What area on this list could most use some improvement?
- What will you do differently before your next meeting?

**Caveats and Considerations:**

- Wherever the word *meeting* exists, a trainer or consultant can substitute *workshop* or *seminar*.

# The Impact of Diversity-Related Variables on Performance Appraisal

| Cultural Factors | Impact on Appraisal | Behavior |
|---|---|---|
| Avoidance of loss of face | Anxiety on the part of the employee and unwillingness to discuss any criticism. | Smiling and laughter may be signs of embarrassment; missing conferences or absenteeism on performance evaluation day may be signs of avoidance. |
| Emphasis on harmony | Agreement to items not clearly understood. | Saying yes even when not understanding or disagreeing. |
| Respect for authority | Unwillingness to question the review or disagree with any points made by the evaluator. | Lack of eye contact and not entering into a dialogue with the boss. |
| External locus of control | Difficulty in seeing the consequences of behavior; not connecting the review with one's own behavior. | Comments may show that the employee does not make the connection between his/her performance and the evaluation ratings. |
| Emphasis on relationship rather than task | Task accomplishment not seen as the critical variable in job success; relationship with boss, seniority, and group status takes precedence. | Attempts to please the boss as well as bewilderment shown by a blank facial expression. |
| Difficulty in separating self from performance | Taking the review personally and finding comments hurtful; "But I thought you liked me" attitude; individual sees criticism as an affront rather than as helpful feedback. | Showing feelings of hurt, betrayal, or embarrassment. |
| Emphasis on group over individual | Difficulty in distinguishing own performance from team's as evaluating individual performance may be a different paradigm for employee used to group results being the focus of evaluation. Calling attention to individual contributions is perceived negatively. Employee may also find calling attention to him/herself awkward and disloyal to co-workers. | Signs of discomfort, confusion, or embarrassment such as smiling, withdrawal, or clamming up. |

**Other Diversity Factors**

| Cultural Factors | Impact on Appraisal | Behavior |
|---|---|---|
| Lack of common base of experience | Employee may feel misunderstood and unfairly judged if evaluator has not had to deal with similar obstacles or outside of work problems (e.g., older worker, single parent, or employee with elder-care responsibilities). | Sulking silence or defensiveness. |
| Previous discrimination | Employees who have experienced discrimination in the past are apt to be mistrustful and skeptical of the value and results of formal appraisal systems. | Lack of participation, sarcasm. |

# Pinpointing Diversity-Related Influences
## that Impact Performance Evaluation

| Cultural/Diversity-Related Factors | Employee's Behavior | Manager's Action |
|---|---|---|
| Avoidance of loss of face | | |
| Emphasis on harmony | | |
| Respect for authority | | |
| External locus of control | | |
| Emphasis on relationship rather than task | | |
| Difficulty in separating self from performance | | |
| Emphasis on group over individual | | |
| Lack of common base of experience | | |
| Previous discrimination | | |

# Suggestions for Using *Pinpointing Diversity-Related Influences that Impact Performance Evaluation*

**Objectives:**

- Identify diversity-related variables affecting performance evaluation.
- Gain information that will help determine actions to take to overcome diversity-related obstacles to performance evaluation effectiveness.

**Intended Audience:**

- Managers wanting to increase effectiveness of performance evaluation with diverse employees.
- Trainees in a managing diversity seminar.

**Processing the Activity:**

- Individuals analyze a recent performance evaluation experience with an employee from a different background using the worksheet. They check any of the variables they perceived as influencing the process, then jot down the employee behaviors that indicated this factor was operating. In the final column, they write any actions the manager could take to improve communication and get buy-in from the employee.
- Small groups can discuss those variables checked and behaviors observed, and then brainstorm additional actions the manager could take.
- The whole group discusses brainstormed suggestions for managers.

**Questions for Discussion:**

- Which variables had the most impact?
- What was the effect these variables had on the performance evaluation?
- What could the manager do to deal with these variables and overcome any potential obstacle?
- What insights have you gained?

**Caveats and Considerations:**

- This worksheet can be used as a coaching tool in helping managers develop more effective performance evaluation skills.
- This worksheet can be used by managers as a planning tool when setting up future performance evaluation sessions.

# Ineffective Sample Performance Evaluation

**I. General Information**

Name _____ Review Period _____

Reviewer _____ Date of Review _____

**II. Performance**

| Objectives | Rating |
|---|---|
| 1. Learn foreign side of business | Exceeds expectations |
| 2. Participate in in-house training | Meets expectations |
| 3. Respond to company reports | Meets expectations |
| 4. Reduce operating costs | Exceeds expectations |

# Effective Sample Performance Evaluation

**I. General Information**

Name _____ Review Period _____

Reviewer _____ Date of Review _____

**II. Performance**

| Objectives | Results Achieved | Rating |
|---|---|---|
| 1. Learn how to contact foreign clients and negotiate international contracts. | Negotiated two successful international contracts. | Exceeds expectations |
| 2. Complete in-house managing diversity seminar and put information to use in own department. | Completed course and made three changes in department due to learning in seminar. | Exceeds expectations |
| 3. Respond via memos to monthly regional reports. | Writes and distributes accurate, informative memos within three days of receiving reports. | Exceeds expectations |
| 4. Reduce departmental operating costs by 5% each year. | Reduced operating costs by 7% by consolidating forms and streamlining reporting procedures. | Exceeds expectations |

# Evaluating Yourself as a Performance Evaluator

|  | Yes | Sometimes | No |
|---|---|---|---|
| 1. I explain the performance expectations of the job to employees. | —— | —— | —— |
| 2. I check employees' understanding of the role and performance expectations. | —— | —— | —— |
| 3. I explain the reasons for performance review to employees, emphasizing benefits to the organization and the individual. | —— | —— | —— |
| 4. I explain the steps in the evaluation process from the setting of standards and the use of forms to the actual evaluation session. | —— | —— | —— |
| 5. I give employees the time and the opportunity to do self-evaluation before the joint session. | —— | —— | —— |
| 6. I listen openly to employees' perceptions of their performance. | —— | —— | —— |
| 7. I remain objective and nondefensive in the session. | —— | —— | —— |
| 8. I observe the employee in action throughout the year and make notes on my observations. | —— | —— | —— |
| 9. I use performance criteria based on observable behaviors and measurable results. | —— | —— | —— |
| 10. I give myself time to prepare the evaluation document with thought and care. | —— | —— | —— |
| 11. I plan the evaluation session, setting it for the most productive time and place. | —— | —— | —— |
| 12. I create a comfortable, inviting climate at the evaluation session. | —— | —— | —— |
| 13. I spend a few minutes initially in the session talking with the employee to break the ice and open communication. | —— | —— | —— |
| 14. I am willing to modify my evaluation, incorporating ideas and comments from the employee's self-evaluation. | —— | —— | —— |
| 15. I require the employee to set his/her own goals and make an action plan for achieving them. | —— | —— | —— |

# Suggestions for Using *Evaluating Yourself as a Performance Evaluator*

## Objectives:

- Assess one's strengths and weaknesses as a performance evaluator.
- Identify behaviors that could enhance one's effectiveness as a performance evaluator.
- Trigger thinking about self-development regarding this management responsibility.

## Intended Audience:

- Managers seeking to increase their effectiveness as performance evaluators.
- Trainees in a managing diversity seminar.

## Processing the Activity:

- Individuals rate themselves by placing checks in the appropriate column on the worksheet.
- Individuals share, in pairs or small groups, their ratings, identifying strengths and weaknesses and discussing potential areas for development, responding to the following questions:
  What did I do well?
  What do I need to work on to do better next time?
  What is one specific way in which I can make the next evaluation more effective?
- Group discusses reactions, insights, and learning.
- Individuals make a contract for self-development by targeting one or two behaviors to work on that would increase their effectiveness as performance evaluators.

## Questions for Discussion:

- Which behaviors are easiest/hardest for you to do?
- What is the consequence of not doing those that are hardest?
- What would be the consequence of incorporating these?
- Which behaviors are you willing to do more often to make your performance evaluations more effective?

## Caveats and Considerations:

- This worksheet can be used one-on-one in coaching sessions with managers as well as in supervisory/management training sessions focusing on performance evaluation.
- It can be used as a self-evaluation tool after each session and as a guide in planning future evaluation conferences.

# Diversity-Related Performance Standards
# for Managers

_____ Hiring, retaining, and promoting individuals from diverse backgrounds.

_____ Coaching and grooming diverse individuals for advancement.

_____ Building cohesive, productive work teams from diverse staffs.

_____ Resolving diversity-related conflicts between staff members.

_____ Maintaining a low rate of discrimination and harassment complaints.

_____ Developing staff through delegation.

_____ Planning and leading effective meetings with a diverse staff.

_____ Learning about the cultural norms and values of employees.

_____ Helping new employees acculturate to the organization's norms.

_____ Providing cultural sensitivity training for staff.

_____ Attending cultural awareness training and applying learning with own staff.

# Suggestions for Using *Diversity-Related Performance Standards for Managers*

## Objectives:

- Identify appropriate performance standards for managers regarding dealing with diversity.
- Assess existing and/or desired practices regarding the management of diversity.
- Assess one's own effectiveness in managing a diverse staff.

## Intended Audience:

- Managers wanting to increase their effectiveness in leading diverse staffs.
- Executives seeking to increase their organization's effectiveness in managing diversity.
- Trainees in a managing diversity seminar.
- Task forces charged with the task of designing performance standards for managers.

## Processing the Activity:

- Individuals can utilize this checklist in a number of ways. They can check those criteria that are presently part of their performance standards. They can star those they think need to be added. Executives can do the same with regard to subordinates' standards. Task forces can be asked to rank order these to identify top-priority criteria. In still another variation, individuals can use these standards to measure their own performance, checking those they do or rating themselves on a scale of 1 to 5 (low to high) on each criterion.
- Groups can discuss their responses, ratings and/or priorities. If they are groups such as task forces making proposals about performance standards by executives deciding on those to be included, they can work toward consensus on a decision.
- Individuals can also identify those performance standards they would like to add to their own review and make plans for their own development in those areas.

## Questions for Discussion:

- Which of these are/are not part of your performance standards? Performance standards in your organization?
- Which do you think should be included in your evaluation? Other managers' evaluations?
- What other performance criteria related to managing a diverse staff would you add?
- Which do you need to work on to be more effective with your team department or work unit?

## Caveats and Considerations:

- This tool can be used as an assessment for individual managers as well as an activity to prime the pump of those designing standards to support organizational strategy regarding the management of diversity.

# Examples of Performance-Based Criteria

The following are suggested performance behavior statements:

b. Dresses in a manner that inspires customer/client confidence in his/her ability.

c. Helps others with work without being asked.
Responds positively to delegated tasks.
Volunteers for task forces and special projects.

d. Completes projects on schedule.
Takes initiative to correct errors, fix equipment, and/or solve problems.

e. Fulfills job responsibilities completely.
Accomplishes assigned tasks within given time frames.

# Symptoms of Inclusivity

Directions: Put a check next to any itmes that currently exist in your company.

_____ Employees are welcome and accepted regardless of life-style variations.

_____ All segments of your population are represented in the executive suite.

_____ Air time at meetings is not dominated by any one group.

_____ Ethnic, racial, and sexual slurs or jokes are not welcome.

_____ Cliquishness between groups is absent.

_____ Variety in dress and grooming is the norm.

_____ Warm, collegial relationships exist between people of diverse backgrounds.

_____ There is sensitivity to and awareness of different religious and ethnic holidays and customs.

_____ Selection of food and refreshments at organizationally sponsored functions or food facilities takes into account religious and personal preferences.

_____ Flexibility exists to accommodate personal responsibilities outside the job.

# Suggestions for Using *Symptoms of Inclusivity*

**Objectives:**

- To assess the openness of your work group or organization.
- To identify a starting point for creating more openness.

**Intended Audience:**

- A CEO or vice president of human resources who wants to stimulate a discussion among executive staff about opening up the organization.
- Managers of work groups who want to create a more open environment among staff.
- Trainers teaching managers to create a more open climate.

**Processing the Activity:**

- Explain the directions as stated in the inventory. Ask each participant to check off those items that indicate inclusivity.
- Put people in pairs or small groups and ask them to discuss the symptoms they see. Suggest illustrating their perceptions with concrete examples.
- Tell participants to use all perceptions, no matter how similar or different, as data for group discussion.
- Bring all the small groups back to the big group. Discuss as a whole.

**Questions for Discussion:**

- Where are your perceptions about symptoms of inclusivity the same as others'? Where are they different? How do you account for the differences?
- Think about the places where your work group or organization lacks openness. What does it cost you in individual and team performance?
- Think about times when you have felt excluded. What has been the impact on your performance?
- If you were to begin creating more openness by focusing on one of these symptoms, what one would you choose?
- What can you do to start the process?

**Caveats and Considerations:**

- Remind participants that culture change is slow. Small starts, reinforced over time, can add up to bigger change, but it won't happen overnight.
- Openness and flexibility need to be modeled. Employees learn behavioral norms more from what you and other leaders do than from what you say.

# Identifying Organizational
# Barriers to Diversity

Directions: Rank the following list of obstacles as they occur in your organization. The most significant obstacle rates a 1 and the least important an 8.

_____   Cost of implementation.

_____   Fear of hiring underskilled, uneducated employees.

_____   Strong belief in a system that favors merit.

_____   Annoyance at reverse discrimination.

_____   Perception that there has been a lot of progress.

_____   Diversity not seen as a top-priority issue.

_____   The need to dismantle existing systems to accommodate diversity.

_____   The sheer size of the organization.

# Suggestions for Using *Identifying Organizational Barriers to Diversity*

### Objectives:

- To identify obstacles that partcipants think prevent the organization from dealing with or paying attention to the issue of diversity.
- To compare perception of various participants to determine consensus on barriers and future courses of action.

### Intended Audience:

- An executive staff willing to work on removing obstacles to becoming a more open organization.
- Top management of a division willing to do the same.
- A change agent who works with top management to identify barriers to diversity.

### Processing the Activity:

- Ask all participants to rank order the obstacles from 1 to 8. Number 1 is the biggest obstacle; number 8 is least important.
- Have participants discuss their responses in groups of 7 to 10 participants. Have the group reach consensus on what the biggest obstacles are and determine a starting point for change.

### Questions for Discussion:

- Are there any barriers you would like to add that were not on the list?
- What is the impact to the organization of not dealing with each of these barriers?
- Based on answers to the last question, which three obstacles are most significant or costly?
- What do you see happening to morale and productivity if you do nothing?
- What needs to happen in order to tear down some of these barriers?
- Where is a good place to begin?

### Caveats and Considerations:

- Make certain in a group of 7 to 10 participants that all participants have their say. Everyone needs to contribute to the discussion.
- Keep asking questions that help participants see the high cost of exclusion.

# How Open to Change Is Your Organizational Culture?

Focus on your organization as you read questions 1 through 15. Then place a check in the appropriate column.

| Questions | Almost Always | Often | Sometimes | Almost Never |
|---|---|---|---|---|
| 1. In my organization, change is viewed as a challenge and an opportunity. | ___ | ___ | ___ | ___ |
| 2. Policies are reviewed annually to assess effectiveness. | ___ | ___ | ___ | ___ |
| 3. Rewards are doled out to suit the preference of the rewardee. | ___ | ___ | ___ | ___ |
| 4. Our personnel department is creative in finding new ways to attract top talent among diverse groups. | ___ | ___ | ___ | ___ |
| 5. There is an openness to suggestions from people at all levels of the organization. | ___ | ___ | ___ | ___ |
| 6. Our strategic plan is evaluated once a year and revised as needed. | ___ | ___ | ___ | ___ |
| 7. "We've always done it that way" is a philosophy that describes my company's response to new ideas. | ___ | ___ | ___ | ___ |
| 8. When problems emerge, there is a willingness to fix them. | ___ | ___ | ___ | ___ |
| 9. Our products and services reflect the awareness of a more diverse consumer base. | ___ | ___ | ___ | ___ |
| 10. My boss values new ideas and implements them quickly. | ___ | ___ | ___ | ___ |
| 11. Performance evaluations in this organization measure an employee's adaptation to change. | ___ | ___ | ___ | ___ |
| 12. Top executives in this company are innovative and approachable. | ___ | ___ | ___ | ___ |
| 13. We can and do make midcourse corrections easily. | ___ | ___ | ___ | ___ |
| 14. There is little variation in style of dress among employees. | ___ | ___ | ___ | ___ |
| 15. People at all levels of the organization are continuously trying to build or rebuild a better mousetrap. | ___ | ___ | ___ | ___ |

# Directions for Scoring *How Open to Change Is Your Organizational Culture?*

| Numbers 1–6, 8–13, and 15 | Almost always | 4 points |
|---|---|---|
| | Often | 3 points |
| | Sometimes | 2 points |
| | Almost never | 1 point |

| Numbers 7 and 14 | Almost always | 1 point |
|---|---|---|
| | Often | 2 points |
| | Sometimes | 3 points |
| | Almost never | 4 points |

1. ____    6. ____    11. ____

2. ____    7. ____    12. ____

3. ____    8. ____    13. ____

4. ____    9. ____    14. ____

5. ____    10. ____    15. ____

Total: ____

**Answer Key**

**50 to 60:** The culture of your organization is open to change. You are able to react and adapt quickly, and are open to new ideas.

**40 to 49:** Your organization understands that change is a reality. In some ways you are open to it, but you haven't fully embraced it, nor are you harnessing change to make it work for you.

**30 to 39:** Your organization understands the value of change, but you need to be more open to its reality and quicker in the implementation process.

**15 to 29:** If you don't get better at adapting, you won't be around long.

## Suggestions for Using *How Open to Change Is Your Organizational Culture?*

### Objectives:

- To help a work group or part of an organization assess how open its culture is to change.
- To identify places where an organization or group is not open.
- To determine what, if anything, needs to be done to make the culture more open and flexible.

### Intended Audience:

- Executive staff conducting its own assessment of the climate.
- An internal or external change agent working with the CEO and executive staff or management staff of any division.
- An internal or external change agent using this assessment at various levels of the organization to gather feedback that can be fed upward to top management and compared against their collective perceptions.

### Processing the Activity:

- Distribute questionnaire to each participant and clearly identify the group being evaluated. Is it the whole organization? One division? A smaller work group?
- Ask participants to check the most appropriate answer for all 15 questions.
- Explain directions for scoring, and ask each participant to come up with a total.
- On a flip chart, record all the scores so the group can get an idea of how varied the perceptions are. There is no need to match names to scores.
- Then, depending on the size of the group, have small-group discussions. Anything from pairs to foursomes is good. Have participants look at their one- and two-point answers.

### Questions for Discussion:

- Look at your one- and two-point answers. What do they indicate about the openness of your culture?
- What areas are ripe for change as you review your responses?
- What are you willing to do to begin the process of becoming more open?

### Caveats and Considerations:

- The higher the level of management acting on data from this questionnaire, the more permeable the culture will be to change.
- This tool can provide valuable feedback from all levels of the organization. How it's presented to top management will influence receptivity. Get their buy-in before you use it.

# Sample Losses and Gains Experienced during Change

| | Losses | Gains |
|---|---|---|
| **Me** | *Career opportunity* | *Marketable experience in managing and functioning in a multicultural work environment* |
| **Organization** | *Low employee morale* | *Creates opportunity to respond to employee needs and increase job satisfaction* |

# Losses and Gains Experienced during Change

|  | **Losses** | **Gains** |
|---|---|---|
| **Me** | | |
| **Organization** | | |

## Suggestions for Using *Losses and Gains Experienced during Change*

### Objectives:

- To foster the idea that change can be positive as well as negative.
- To help people impacted by change get a broader perspective and thereby lessen the stress and resistance.
- To explore with co-workers different views of change and the gains/losses that accompany it.

### Intended Audience:

- Managers helping individuals or a work group adjust to change.
- Any training professional who needs to do a seminar on change.
- Internal or external consultants who have to help resistant work groups or organizations deal with change and move beyond resistance.

### Processing the Activity:

- In each of the four quadrants, have participants list perceived losses and gains for themselves and the organization.
- In pairs, have participants discuss their losses and gains in each area.
- On a flip chart and easel, list the losses and gains from the random responses of group members.
- Conduct a discussion with the whole group about the data that surface.

### Questions for Discussion:

- What losses have you experienced for yourself? The organization?
- What gains in each category?
- What strikes you about these lists?
- What can you take from this experience to the next change?

### Caveats and Considerations:

- There will be some participants who adamantly refuse to see any positive element in some of their changes. Acknowledge their anger and accept their feelings or reactions.

# Common Career Assumptions

In order to start assessing your assumptions, look at the seven samples below and circle any that are appropriate for you.

1.  If I am competent and work hard, I will get ahead.

2.  If I am loyal to the organization, it will be loyal to me.

3.  There is a lifetime commitment between me and the organization.

4.  The organization will take care of me (e.g., benefits, vacations, sick time).

5.  People will be judged by the job they do.

6.  The organization will remain stable enough that I can accomplish the career goals I've set.

7.  I will work with people who share my values and life-style.

**Some of Your Career Assumptions**

Once you have circled the career assumptions listed above that apply to you, write any other relevant career assumptions that are appropriate.

1.  _____

2.  _____

3.  _____

As you look at your assumptions, see which ones need to change in order to accurately reflect today's changing reality. Here's how to do this exercise, using the first two assumptions as examples.

**Assumption:**   If I am competent and work hard, I will get ahead.
**Accurate rewrite:**   If I am competent and work hard, I may get ahead, but nothing is certain.

**Assumption:**   If I am loyal to the organization, it will be loyal to me.
**Accurate rewrite:**   The organization and I will have a mutually satisfying relationship so long as it meets both our needs.

Now, take three of your assumptions. First, write each assumption as you have held it. Then rewrite each to reflect today's reality.

Currently held assumption:

_____

_____

Rewritten assumption:

_____

_____

Currently held assumption:

_____

_____

Rewritten assumption:

_____

_____

Currently held assumption:

_____

_____

Rewritten assumption:

_____

_____

# Suggestions for Using *Common Career Assumptions*

## Objectives:

- To help participants rethink their basic assumptions and expectations about work.
- To provide insight about the subtler changes in expectations and the anger or frustration that can result from a "broken contract."

## Intended Audience:

- Anyone in any organization who is trying to deal with losses from change.
- HR practitioners and trainers trying to help organizations through downsizing efforts.
- Managers trying to help their own work groups through rapid change in organizations that are downsizing or involved in other changes.

## Processing the Activity:

- Ask participants to look at the list of common career assumptions listed in the learning activity and list any others they would add.
- Rewrite the assumptions to accurately reflect today's reality.

## Questions for Discussion:

- Which work-world myths have to go by the wayside?
- How do you feel about the changing reality?
- How long ago did this reality change?
- What can help you come to terms with this new reality?
- What is the relevance of this process to you or your work group as you deal with future change?

## Caveats and Considerations:

- Focus your discussion on subtle change and the betrayal you feel when unwritten contracts or expectations are violated.
- Help participants see that the new expectation, constant change, has an upside and a downside. They can make change work for them.

# Dealing with the Losses from Change

Directions: Think about the diversity you and your work group are dealing with. In the boxes below, make notes about how this loss impacts both you and your group.

| Loss | Impact on You | Impact on Your Work Group |
|------|---------------|---------------------------|
| 1. Attachment | | |
| 2. Turf | | |
| 3. Structure | | |
| 4. Future | | |
| 5. Meaning | | |
| 6. Control | | |

Source: William Bridges, *Surviving Corporate Transition* (New York: Doubleday, 1988).

# Suggestions for Using *Dealing with the Losses from Change*

## Objectives:

- To help individuals and work groups identify the losses they experience from rapid change.

## Intended Audience:

- Trainers and managers who can help individual employees and work groups deal with the frustration, stress, and anger sometimes associated with change.

## Processing the Activity:

- Ask participants to write down perceived losses as an individual and as a member of a group.
- In pairs or small groups, have people discuss their comments.
- Discuss perceptions among the whole group, looking both for common viewpoints of loss as well as different reactions.

## Questions for Discussion:

- Where do you feel the greatest loss personally? In the work group?
- Were there some areas where you felt no loss?
- What was your reaction to writing this down and seeing your thoughts on paper?
- What were the most interesting reactions that surfaced in your group? Any surprises?
- Based on comments you heard from others, are there any of your losses you are willing to rethink? If so, which ones?
- How can you use this mental process next time you feel a loss?

## Caveats and Considerations:

- People have strong feelings about these losses. Provide enough time for venting and good discussion.
- Create a trusting climate, but suggest people group themselves with those they don't know too well in the discussion segment. It might offer a varied perspective.

# Stages of Integration

**Stage 1 Behavior:
Rejection/Resistance**

Characterized by fear of
acculturation due to
sublimating one's culture.
The stakes for belonging
are seen as too high.

**Stage 2 Behavior:
Isolation**

Characterized by physical
and psychological
withdrawal. There is a
perfunctory politeness,
but superficial interaction.

**Stage 3 Behavior:
Assimilation**

Characterized by
adjustments toward group
norms. There is a clarity
about the operating rules.

**Stage 4 Behavior:
Coexistence**

Characterized by an
ability to become part of
the mainstream while
maintaining sense of self
and uniqueness.

**Stage 5 Behavior:
Integration**

Characterized by a sense
of belonging.
Relationships are real and
fluid and involve conflict
and cooperation.

Source: Adapted from Eileen Morley, "Management Integration," paper presented at OD '80—A Conference on Current Theory and Practice in Organizational Development, San Diego, 1980.

# Assessment Methods Compared

| Method | Advantage | Disadvantage |
|---|---|---|
| Questionnaire | Data can be obtained from every-one in the organization in a cost-effective way.<br>Data are collected anonymously so employees feel free to be more honest.<br>Provides data in comparative form from all respondents that can be quantified and statistically ana-lyzed.<br>Takes relatively little time from employees and can be done si-multaneously in many locations.<br>Simple to administer. | Requires literacy and possibly translations into other languages<br>One-way communication offers no way to get clarification or expla-nation about responses.<br>Responses tend to be limited by information requested in ques-tionnaire.<br>May get lip service and perfunc-tory answers rather than thoughtful responses.<br>Impersonality and lack of human touch may put off employees, es-pecially those from other cultures. |
| Interviews | Interviewees may feel freer to speak openly without others present.<br>Problems and issues surfaced can be explored in depth.<br>Permits collection of examples, anecdotes, and stories that illus-trate the issues and put them in human terms.<br>More personal touch allows for person-to-person communica-tion. | Least time-efficient and most costly method.<br>Requires skilled interviewer to guide sessions.<br>Data collected from a limited num-ber of people may provide a nar-row slice of information if only staff at certain levels are inter-viewed.<br>Affects the least number of staff so may generate only limited commitment. |
| Focus Groups | Serve as a teaching tool, building respondee awareness about di-versity.<br>Produce richer data through in-depth discussions about topics and issues.<br>Two-way communication permits clarification and explanation of information given.<br>More personal and human.<br>Subtle information from nonverbal clues and body language can be picked up.<br>More time-efficient to get informa-tion from groups rather than in-dividuals one at a time.<br>Interaction generates more data. Comments spark other ideas so new information may emerge.<br>Participants' hearing of each oth-ers' views may expand their un-derstanding of the issues. | Require skilled facilitation in ses-sions.<br>Generally only provide a sample of views, not everyone's.<br>Peer pressure may influence parti-cipants' comments.<br>Takes time to coordinate sessions and schedule the pulling of em-ployees from jobs.<br>People may be uncomfortable in a new setting and an unfamiliar experience.<br>Participants may be reluctant to open up and speak freely for fear of repercussions or because of cultural norms that discourage negative or critical comments. |

# Managing Diversity Questionnaire

|  | Very True | Somewhat True | Not True |
|---|---|---|---|
| In this organization: | | | |
| 1. I am at ease with people of diverse backgrounds. | _____ | _____ | _____ |
| 2. There is diverse staff at all levels. | _____ | _____ | _____ |
| 3. Managers have a track record of hiring and promoting diverse employees. | _____ | _____ | _____ |
| 4. In general, I find change stimulating, exciting, and challenging. | _____ | _____ | _____ |
| 5. Racial, ethnic, and gender jokes are tolerated in the informal environment. | _____ | _____ | _____ |
| 6. Managers hold all people equally accountable. | _____ | _____ | _____ |
| 7. I know about the cultural norms of different groups. | _____ | _____ | _____ |
| 8. The formation of ethnic and gender support groups is encouraged. | _____ | _____ | _____ |
| 9. Managers are flexible, structuring benefits and rules that work for everyone. | _____ | _____ | _____ |
| 10. I am afraid to disagree with members of other groups for fear of being called prejudiced. | _____ | _____ | _____ |
| 11. There is a mentoring program that identifies and prepares women and people of color for promotion. | _____ | _____ | _____ |
| 12. Appreciation of differences can be seen in the rewards managers give. | _____ | _____ | _____ |
| 13. I feel there is more than one right way to do things. | _____ | _____ | _____ |
| 14. Members of the nondominant group feel they belong. | _____ | _____ | _____ |
| 15. One criterion of a manager's performance review is developing the diversity of his/her staff. | _____ | _____ | _____ |
| 16. I think that diverse viewpoints make for creativity. | _____ | _____ | _____ |
| 17. There is high turnover among women and people of color. | _____ | _____ | _____ |
| 18. Managers give feedback and evaluate performance so employees don't "lose face." | _____ | _____ | _____ |
| 19. I am aware of my own assumptions and stereotypes. | _____ | _____ | _____ |

# Managing Diversity Questionnaire (concluded)

|  | Very True | Somewhat True | Not True |
|---|---|---|---|
| 20. Policies are flexible enough to accommodate everyone. | _____ | _____ | _____ |
| 21. Managers get active participation from all employees in meetings. | _____ | _____ | _____ |
| 22. I think there is enough common ground to hold staff together. | _____ | _____ | _____ |
| 23. The speaking of other languages is forbidden. | _____ | _____ | _____ |
| 24. Multicultural work teams function harmoniously. | _____ | _____ | _____ |
| 25. Staff members spend their lunch hour and breaks in mixed groups. | _____ | _____ | _____ |
| 26. Money and time are spent on diversity development activities. | _____ | _____ | _____ |
| 27. Managers effectively use problem-solving skills to deal with language differences or other culture clashes. | _____ | _____ | _____ |
| 28. I feel that working in a diverse staff enriches me. | _____ | _____ | _____ |
| 29. Top management backs up its value on diversity with action. | _____ | _____ | _____ |
| 30. Managers have effective strategies to use when one group refuses to work with another. | _____ | _____ | _____ |

**Scoring:**

Items 5, 10, 17, and 23: Very true = 0 points, Somewhat true = 1 point, Not true = 2 points.
  All other items: Very true = 2 points, Somewhat true = 1 point, Not true = 0 points.

_____ Individual attitudes and beliefs: Items 1, 4, 7, 10, 13, 16, 19, 22, 25, 28
_____ Organizational values and norms: Items 2, 5, 8, 11, 14, 17, 20, 23, 26, 29
_____ Management practices and policies: Items 3, 6, 9, 12, 15, 18, 21, 24, 27, 30
_____ Total score

# Suggestions for Using the *Managing Diversity Questionnaire*

**Objectives:**

- Assess three levels of an organization's effectiveness in managing a diverse work force: individual attitudes, organizational values, and management practices.
- Increase awareness and knowledge about aspects of managing diversity.
- Target areas of needed development.

**Intended Audience:**

- Staff at all levels in an organization that is working to increase effectiveness in managing diversity and that desires to understand perceptions of employees about the issues.
- Executive and/or middle management involved in planning diversity development strategies.
- Executive staff members charged with organizational strategy regarding diversity.
- Trainees in a managing diversity seminar.

**Processing the Activity:**

- Individuals are asked to respond to the questionnaire based on their perceptions of the organization and how it functions. They are told that responses are anonymous and are asked to be candid. They are also told how the data generated will be used, who will see them, and what will be done with them.
- Questionnaires are collected and scored.
- Data are compiled and analyzed by item, by the three levels of functioning, and by demographic groupings of staff.
- Data are reported to appropriate executive and or management staff, and a summary of findings is communicated to all participants along with an indication of next steps.

**Questions for Discussion:**

- What are our organization's strengths and weaknesses?
- How similar or disparate are perceptions of different groups, divisions, or levels within the organization?
- What issues need further investigation or clarification?
- What issues need attention?
- Who or what (positions, levels) needs to be involved in dealing with the issues surfaced?

**Caveats and Considerations:**

- Do not embark on a process of this type until you have a clear plan about how the data will be used and a commitment that they will be considered in planning.
- This questionnaire can be used as an awareness builder for managers who want to increase their own effectiveness and/or for those involved in diversity task forces. It can also be used as a jumping-off point for discussions about managing diversity in execution and/or management staff meetings.
- Questionnaires can be coded by level, department, length of time with the company, type of work, and so on to give more specific categories for analysis.

# Symptoms of Diversity-Related Problems:
## Internal Checklist

Check any of the following situations you notice and/or are experiencing in your organization:

_____ Lack of a diverse staff at all levels in the organization.

_____ Complaints about staff speaking other languages on the job.

_____ Resistance to working with or making negative comments about another group (ethnic, racial, cultural, gender, religion, sexual orientation, or physical ability).

_____ Difficulty in communicating due to limited or heavily accented English.

_____ Ethnic, racial, or gender slurs or jokes.

_____ EEOC suits or complaints about discrimination in promotions, pay, and performance reviews.

_____ Lack of social interaction between members of diverse groups.

_____ Increase in grievances by members of nonmainstream groups.

_____ Difficulty in recruiting and retaining members of different groups.

_____ Open conflict between groups or between individuals from different groups.

_____ Mistakes and productivity problems due to employees not understanding directions.

_____ Perceptions that individuals are not valued for their unique contributions.

_____ Ostracism of individuals who are different from the norm.

_____ Barriers in promotion for diverse employees.

_____ Frustrations and irritations resulting from cultural differences.

_____ Other diversity-related problems. Explain: _____

## Suggestions for Using *Symptoms of Diversity-Related Problems: Internal Checklist*

**Objectives:**

- Identify diversity-related problems within the organization.
- Raise awareness and spark discussion about such issues.
- Provide a jumping-off point for taking action to deal with diversity-related problems.

**Intended Audience:**

- Managers, supervisors, and first-line staff in a diverse organization.
- Trainees at a managing diversity seminar.
- Executive staff attempting to identify obstacles to productivity and morale.
- Human resource staff attempting to reduce turnover and grievances.

**Processing the Activity:**

- Individuals are asked to check any of the problems they have experienced within the organization. They may also add others that are not listed.
- Groups can discuss problems checked to get an idea about which issues seem to be most prevalent. They may also assign priorities regarding dealing with the problems, discuss how widespread the problems are, and/or determine which parts of the organization seem to be most affected by particular issues.
- Follow-up will depend on the group involved. Data can be used by managers in solving the problems in their own departments/divisions. They can be used by executives in developing or modifying plans or policies. They can also be used by human resource staff in making recommendations to executive management and in modifying their own procedures. Finally, data can be used in planning management development activities.

**Questions for Discussion:**

- What seem to be the most frequent problems surfaced?
- How widespread are they? Which sections of the organization seem most affected?
- What is the cost to the organization of these problems? What will happen if these go unaddressed?
- What additional information do we need in order to address these? From whom?
- Where/how do these issues need to be dealt with?
- What do we need to do to address these problems?
- What support, skills, and training do managers need to deal with these issues?
- What organization systems or policies need to be examined and possibly modified?

**Caveats and Considerations:**

- Be careful not to make any premature commitments regarding actions to ad-

# Stages of Diversity Survey:
# An Organizational Progress Report

Directions: Check each response that is true of your organization. You may check more than one response for each item number.

1. **In this organization:**

   _____**a.** There is a standard way to dress and look.

   _____**b.** While there is no dress code, most employees dress within a conventional range.

   _____**c.** There is much variety in employees' style of dress.

2. **In this organization:**

   _____**a.** Newcomers are expected to adapt to existing norms.

   _____**b.** There is some flexibility to accommodate the needs of diverse employees.

   _____**c.** Norms are flexible enough to include everyone.

3. **In this organization:**

   _____**a.** Diversity is an issue that stirs irritation and resentment.

   _____**b.** Attention is paid to meeting EEO requirements and affirmative action quotas.

   _____**c.** Working toward a diverse staff at all levels is seen as a strategic advantage.

4. **In this organization, dealing with diversity is:**

   _____**a.** Not a top priority.

   _____**b.** The responsibility of the human resource department.

   _____**c.** Considered a part of every manager's job.

5. **People in this organization:**

   _____**a.** Downplay or ignore differences among employees.

   _____**b.** Tolerate differences and the needs they imply.

   _____**c.** Value differences and see diversity as an advantage to be cultivated.

6. **Demographics of this organization show that:**

   _____**a.** There is diversity among staff at lower levels.

   _____**b.** There is diverse staff at lower and middle levels.

   _____**c.** There is diversity at all levels of the organization.

7. **Money is spent on training programs to help employees:**

   _____**a.** Adapt to the organization's culture and learn "the way we do things here."

   _____**b.** Develop diverse staff's ability to move up the organization ladder.

   _____**c.** Communicate effectively across gender and cultural barriers.

# Stages of Diversity Survey:
## An Organizational Progress Report (concluded)

8. **Managers are held accountable for:**

_____**a.** Motivating staff and increasing productivity.

_____**b.** Avoiding EEO and discrimination grievances and suits.

_____**c.** Working effectively with a diverse staff.

9. **Managers are held accountable for:**

_____**a.** Maintaining a stable staff and perpetuating existing norms.

_____**b.** Meeting affirmative action goals and identifying promotable talent.

_____**c.** Building productive work teams with diverse staff.

10. **Managers are rewarded for:**

_____**a.** Following existing procedures.

_____**b.** Solving problems in the system.

_____**c.** Initiating creative programs and trying new methods.

11. **This organization:**

_____**a.** Resists change and seeks to maintain the status quo.

_____**b.** Deals with changes as they occur.

_____**c.** Is continually working on improvement.

12. **In this organization, it is an advantage to:**

_____**a.** Be a white male.

_____**b.** Learn to be like the "old guard."

_____**c.** Be unique and find new ways of doing things.

**Directions for Scoring:**
Count the total number of checks next to each letter (a, b, c) and fill in the totals below:

_____ **a.** Monocultural
_____ **b.** Nondiscriminitory
_____ **c.** Multicultural

# Suggestions for Using the *Stages of Diversity Survey: An Organizational Progress Report*

## Objectives:

- Determine an organization's stage of development in dealing with diversity.
- Give feedback to executive management about the organization's status regarding dealing with diversity.
- Provide data for strategizing regarding organization development.

## Intended Audience:

- Middle- to lower-level staff in a diverse organization.
- Management and supervisory staff.
- Members of diversity task forces or planning teams.
- Executive staff involved in strategic planning.

## Processing the Activity:

- Individuals are asked to check each response that they perceive as a true statement about the organization. They may check more than one response for each item.
- Questionnaires are collected and scored. If used by a task force or planning team, they may be scored in the group.
- Scores are analyzed, and data are interpreted and then presented to planning group.

## Questions for Discussion:

- Where is our organization in its development regarding diversity?
- What surprises or new information is there?
- What issues are uncovered that need to be addressed?
- What kind of planning or development is indicated for growth?

## Caveats and Considerations:

- While this instrument leads to a score that places the organization in a particular stage of development, its purpose is not to label the organization but rather to serve as a tool for exploration and growth. Help those with the information utilize it for that purpose.
- Individuals may disagree with some of the statements. They may also find some indicators of particular stages not desirable. In these cases, use disagreement to provoke discussion of desired organization goals and indicators of their achievements.

# Diversity Awareness Continuum

Directions: Put an *X* that represents where you fit along the dotted line for each continuum below.

| | | |
|---|---|---|
| I am not knowledgeable about the cultural norms of different groups in the organization. | .................................................. | I am knowledgeable about the cultural norms of different groups in the organization. |
| I do not hold stereotypes about other groups. | .................................................. | I admit my stereotypes about other groups. |
| I feel partial to, and more comfortable with, some groups than others. | .................................................. | I feel equally comfortable with all groups. |
| I gravitate toward others who are like me. | .................................................. | I gravitate toward others who are different. |
| I find it more satisfying to manage a homogeneous team. | .................................................. | I find it more satisfying to manage a multicultural team. |
| I feel that everyone is the same, with similar values and preferences. | .................................................. | I feel that everyone is unique, with differing values and preferences. |
| I am perplexed by the culturally different behaviors I see among staff. | .................................................. | I understand the cultural influences that are at the root of some of the behaviors I see. |
| I react with irritation when confronted with someone who does not speak English. | .................................................. | I show patience and understanding with limited English speakers. |
| I am task focused and don't like to waste time chatting. | .................................................. | I find that more gets done when I spend time on relationships first. |
| I feel that newcomers to this society should adapt to our rules. | .................................................. | I feel that both newcomers and the organizations in which they work need to change to fit together. |

Draw your profile by connecting your *X*s. The closer your line is to the right-hand column, the greater your awareness regarding diversity. The closer to the left-hand column, the less aware you may be about diversity-related issues.

## Suggestions for Using the *Diversity Awareness Continuum*

**Objectives:**

* Assess individual awareness and attitudes about diversity.
* Give management information about staff attitudes and potential sources of resistance to diversity.
* Give individuals information about potential areas of personal/professional development.

**Intended Audience:**

* Members of diverse and/or changing work teams.
* Managers dealing with diverse staffs.
* Trainees in diversity awareness and managing diversity seminars.

**Processing the Activity:**

* Individuals place an *X* representing where they fit along each continuum on the sheet. They then connect their *X*s.
* In groups or in a team, they discuss their responses, focusing on the farthest left and farthest right marks. Discussion continues about reactions and feelings about diversity and consequences of those reactions.
* Individuals target one or two areas for personal development.

**Questions for Discussion:**

* Where are you most/least aware and knowledgeable about diversity?
* What do you need to learn?
* Where are your greatest strengths? Weaknesses?
* What are the team's/group's greatest strengths of weaknesses regarding diversity?
* What do you need to do as a team to grow? As an individual?

**Caveats and Considerations:**

* In addition to its value as a tool for growth for the individual and team, this activity can provide data to training and development professionals developing diversity training programs.
* It also serves as a subtle teaching tool, suggesting areas of development regarding diversity.

# Diversity Opinionnaire

Please respond with a rating that represents your feelings about each opinion below. 5 = strongly agree, 4 = agree, 3 = uncertain, 2 = disagree, 1 = strongly disagree.

_____ 1. Everyone who works in this organization should be required to speak English.

_____ 2. Diversity brings creativity and energy to a work group.

_____ 3. Immigrants should be expected to forsake their own cultures and adapt to American ways.

_____ 4. Multicultural teams can be stimulating, productive, and fun.

_____ 5. People should leave their differences at home and conform to organizational standards at work.

_____ 6. Showing flexibility and accommodation to people's individual needs and preferences increases commitment and motivation.

_____ 7. Diversity only brings unnecessary conflict and problems to a work group.

_____ 8. Women and people of color are underrepresented at higher levels in this organization.

_____ 9. Increasing work-force diversity has led to a decline in quality.

_____ 10. People are more motivated and productive when they feel they are accepted for who they are.

_____ 11. Women and minorities are oversensitive to prejudice and discrimination.

_____ 12. Stereotypes exist about all groups.

_____ 13. Minorities tend to stick together.

_____ 14. Differences often make people uncomfortable.

_____ 15. Some groups are more suited for or talented at certain jobs.

_____ 16. There should be no double standards. The rules should be the same for everyone, regardless of gender, race, age, ethnicity, and so on.

_____ 17. America would be a better place if people would assimilate into one culture.

_____ 18. America would be a better place if people were allowed to preserve their individual cultures.

_____ 19. People are reluctant to disagree with minority group employees for fear of being called prejudiced.

_____ 20. Training is needed to help employees understand each other and overcome communication barriers.

**Scoring:**

_____ Total score for odd-numbered items
_____ Total score for even-numbered items

# Suggestions for Using the *Diversity Opinionnaire*

**Objectives:**

- Assess attitudes about openness toward diversity.
- Identify potential sources of resistance to diversity.
- Uncover personal prejudices and feelings about diversity.

**Intended Audience:**

- Staff at all levels in a diverse organization.
- Managers dealing with a diverse staff.
- Trainees in a diversity awareness or managing diversity seminar.
- Individuals wanting to increase their own awareness and sensitivity regarding dealing with differences.
- Members of a diversity task force or planning group needing to "get their own house in order" before working with the organization about this issue.

**Processing the Activity:**

- Individuals respond by assigning a number, from 1 to 5, to each of the statements.
- If used as an organization assessment, questionnaires are collected, scores are tabulated and analyzed, and then data are reported to the appropriate planning group.
- If used by individuals or groups for their own information and growth, individuals score their own, then discuss results and their significance.
- Individuals can target areas for personal growth, while teams or groups can pinpoint areas for group development.

**Questions for Discussion:**

- What is the workplace impact of these attitudes?
- How can these opinions affect relationships with diverse groups?
- How do they affect manager/subordinate relationships?
- Which attitudes represent obstacles to making diversity an asset to the organization or team?
- What needs to be done to deal with these perceptions? How?

**Caveats and Considerations:**

- Discussion is apt to be heated, and there may be a tendency for individuals to want to defend their opinion, attack another's, and/or argue for their own point of view. It is important to remind people that attitudes and perceptions are neither right nor wrong; however, they are realities for those holding them. Keep the discussion centered on the effect of the attitudes and the consequences of the behaviors they provoke. Focus on the cost to the organization, team, and individual.

# Staff Diversity Needs Analysis

Please respond to the questions below by answering *true* or *false*.

_____ 1. I am comfortable working with individuals who are different from me in race and cultural background.

_____ 2. I am sometimes confused by the behavior of employees from different backgrounds.

_____ 3. It is difficult for me to understand people who speak with thick accents.

_____ 4. I'm reluctant to disagree with employees of different groups for fear of being considered prejudiced.

_____ 5. I know about my own cultural background and how it influences my behavior.

_____ 6. I am able to resolve conflicts with employees who are different from me in cultural background, gender, race, and life-style.

_____ 7. My behavior is influenced by gender differences.

_____ 8. Prejudice exists in every individual.

_____ 9. I feel comfortable talking about differences in race, culture, and sexual orientation.

_____ 10. Racial and cultural differences influence my behavior.

_____ 11. Stereotypes are held about every group.

_____ 12. I'm not sure what labels to use in referring to different groups.

_____ 13. My behavior is influenced by differences in sexual orientation.

_____ 14. I understand the different cultural influences of my co-workers.

_____ 15. I get frustrated when communicating with limited-English-speaking individuals.

_____ 16. I am most comfortable spending time with people who are similar to me in background.

_____ 17. I find the behaviors of some members of diverse groups irritating.

_____ 18. I'm fearful of offending individuals of diverse groups by saying the wrong thing.

_____ 19. People of diverse groups are treated differently because they act differently.

_____ 20. I find myself thinking, "Why don't they act like us?"

# Staff Diversity Needs Analysis (concluded)

_____ 21.  I'm able to resolve problems easily with co-workers who are different from me.

_____ 22.  I recognize my own biases and prejudices.

_____ 23.  Certain behaviors of diverse groups bother me.

_____ 24.  I am able to work with people so I feel I fit in, no matter how different we are.

_____ 25.  I wish we were all more the same.

_____ 26.  I understand some of the reasons why there is cultural clash and conflicts between groups.

_____ 27.  When dealing with differences, I am able to "walk in someone else's shoes."

_____ 28.  I find differences among us interesting and stimulating.

_____ 29.  I understand the reasons for my own reactions to others' differentness.

_____ 30.  I find many similarities between me and my diverse co-workers.

**Scoring**—Give each answer a point value as follows:

Items 1, 5, 6, 7, 8, 9, 10, 11, 13, 14, 21, 22, 24, 26, 27, 28, 29, 30: True = 1 point, False = 0 points.
Items 2, 3, 4, 12, 15, 16, 17, 18, 19, 20, 23, 25: True = 0 points, False = 1 point.

_____  Awareness = Total score for items 1, 4, 7, 10, 13, 16, 19, 22, 25, 28
_____  Knowledge = Total score for items 2, 5, 8, 11, 14, 17, 20, 23, 26, 29
_____  Skills = Total score for items 3, 6, 9, 12, 15, 18, 21, 24, 27, 30
_____  Total

# Suggestions for Using the *Staff Diversity Needs Analysis*

## Objectives:

- Identify training and development needs of staff regarding diversity.
- Pinpoint specific areas for development.
- Give information to individuals regarding personal training and/or development needs.

## Intended Audience:

- Staff at nonmanagerial levels in a diverse organization.
- Trainees in a diversity training seminar.
- Individuals wanting to increase their own ability to deal with diversity.

## Processing the Activity:

- Individuals respond to the statements by marking them true or false.
- Questionnaires can be collected and scored for use as a training needs assessment.
- Questionnaires can be scored by the individuals, then discussed in groups. Discussion can focus on strengths and weaknesses and areas of needed growth.
- Individuals can prioritize needs and target specific areas for growth.
- Training and development professionals can analyze scores to determine appropriate training content and design.

## Questions for Discussion:

- What strengths and weaknesses emerge?
- Where are the greatest growth needs—awareness, knowledge, and/or skills?
- How do weaknesses in these areas affect productivity? Morale? Service?
- What does this tell us about training needed by staff in specific departments/ units?
- What do we need to find out more about?

## Caveats and Considerations:

- This questionnaire can serve as a catalyst for discussion within a team dealing with diversity. The group can identify collective weaknesses and target areas for growth and development.

# Management Development Diversity Needs Analysis

Please respond to the questions below by answering *true* or *false*.

——— 1.  I am comfortable managing individuals who are different from me in race and cultural background.

——— 2.  I am sometimes confused by the behavior of employees from different backgrounds.

——— 3.  I'm able to resolve problems easily with employees on my staff who are different from me.

——— 4.  I'm reluctant to disagree with employees of different groups for fear of being considered prejudiced.

——— 5.  I know about my own cultural background and how it influences my behavior and my expectations of employees.

——— 6.  I know how to give feedback so employees of different cultures don't "lose face."

——— 7.  My behavior toward employees is influenced by gender differences.

——— 8.  Prejudice exists in every individual.

——— 9.  I feel comfortable talking with my staff about differences in race, culture, and sexual orientation.

——— 10.  My behavior toward my staff is influenced by racial and cultural differences.

——— 11.  Stereotypes are held about every group.

——— 12.  I am able to give constructive performance reviews with employees of different groups.

——— 13.  My behavior toward my staff is influenced by differences in sexual orientation.

——— 14.  I understand the different cultural influences of the people I manage or supervise.

——— 15.  I get frustrated when my staff segregates into subgroups along cultural or racial lines.

——— 16.  I am most comfortable managing people who are similar to me in background.

——— 17.  I find the behaviors of some members of diverse groups on my staff irritating.

——— 18.  I'm fearful of offending employees of diverse groups by saying the wrong thing.

——— 19.  People of diverse groups are treated differently because they act differently.

——— 20.  I find myself thinking, "Why don't they act like us?"

# Management Development Diversity Needs Analysis
## (*concluded*)

_____ 21.  It is difficult for me to manage people who speak with thick accents.

_____ 22.  I recognize my own biases and prejudices.

_____ 23.  Certain behaviors of diverse groups on my staff bother me.

_____ 24.  I am able to resolve conflicts between employees of different cultural backgrounds, genders, races, and life-styles.

_____ 25.  I wish my staff were all more the same.

_____ 26.  I understand some of the reasons why there is culture clash and conflicts between employees and groups of employees.

_____ 27.  I'm not sure what labels to use in referring to different groups.

_____ 28.  I find differences among us interesting and stimulating.

_____ 29.  I understand the reasons for my own reactions to others' differentness.

_____ 30.  I am able to build a cohesive work team from my diverse staff.

**Scoring**—Give each answer a point value as follows:

Items 1, 3, 5, 6, 7, 8, 9, 10, 11, 12, 13, 14, 22, 24, 26, 28, 29, 30: True = 1 point, False = 0 points.
Items 2, 4, 15, 16, 17, 18, 19, 20, 21, 23, 25, 27: True = 0 points, False = 1 point.

_____ Awareness = Total score for items 1, 4, 7, 10, 13, 16, 19, 22, 25, 28

_____ Knowledge = Total score for items 2, 5, 8, 11, 14, 17, 20, 23, 26, 29

_____ Skills = Total score for items 3, 6, 9, 12, 15, 18, 21, 24, 27, 30

_____ Total

# Suggestions for Using the *Management Development Diversity Needs Analysis*

## Objectives:

- Identify management development needs regarding diversity.
- Pinpoint specific areas for training.
- Give information to individual managers regarding personal development needs.

## Intended Audience:

- Managers dealing with a diverse work force.
- Trainees in a management development series or a managing diversity seminar.
- Management teams wanting to increase their effectiveness in dealing with diversity.

## Processing the Activity:

- Individuals respond to the statements by marking them true or false.
- Questionnaires can be collected and scored for use as a management development needs assessment by the training department.
- Questionnaires can be scored by individuals, then discussed in groups. Discussion can focus on strengths, weaknesses, and areas of needed growth.
- Groups and individuals within them can prioritize needs and target specific areas for growth. They can even brainstorm ways to accomplish that growth.
- Training and development professionals can analyze scores to determine appropriate training content and design.

## Questions for Discussion:

- What strengths and weaknesses emerge?
- How do the weaknesses impact management effectiveness? Productivity? Morale?
- Where are the greatest growth needs in general areas (awareness, knowledge, skills) and/or specific issues (e.g., communication with limited-English-speaking staff).
- Where do we need to focus our own development?

## Caveats and Considerations:

- Dealing with the issues in this questionnaire may provoke heated discussion if there has been no previous groundwork laid regarding managing diversity. This is best used after a general session discussing changes in work force demographics where venting can be done and where executive management explains organizational goals and strategy regarding diversity.

# Management Development Diversity
# Needs Assessment Checklist

Check any of the following you would like to learn more about.

_____ Understanding attitudes about race, culture, gender, sexual orientation.

_____ Dealing with prejudice and stereotyping.

_____ Understanding norms, practices, and values of different cultures.

_____ Understanding communication differences among groups.

_____ Learning to reward appropriately amid diversity.

_____ Using nondiscriminatory language and labels.

_____ Communicating with limited-English-speaking individuals.

_____ Motivating effectively in a diverse environment.

_____ Resolving cross-cultural conflicts.

_____ Dealing with prejudice on my staff.

_____ Building multicultural work teams.

_____ Giving feedback in culturally sensitive ways.

_____ Enhancing trust in a diverse staff.

_____ Communicating more effectively with diverse employees.

_____ Coaching, grooming, and mentoring diverse employees.

_____ Conducting productive performance reviews with diverse staff.

_____ Recognizing the special needs of different groups.

_____ Creating an environment where all employees feel included.

_____ Other: _____

# Suggestions for Using the *Management Development Diversity Needs Assessment Checklist*

### Objectives:

- Identify management development needs regarding diversity.
- Give information to training and development professionals regarding perceived needs.
- Increase awareness about skills and knowledge essential in managing a diverse staff.

### Intended Audience:

- Managers and supervisors dealing with diverse staffs.
- Potential trainees in a managing diversity seminar.
- Executive staff wanting to increase the effectiveness of managers and supervisors in dealing with diverse staffs.

### Processing the Activity:

- Managers check those aspects of managing diversity in which they need development.
- Groups can discuss items checked and assign priorities to them.
- Training and development staff can then use this information in planning training for managers.
- Executive staff can discuss data and assign priorities for management training.

### Questions for Discussion:

- Which items were checked?
- What themes or issues do these items relate to?
- What is the effect of these deficiencies on the job?
- What are the consequences if these go unaddressed?
- Which are most/least widespread? Critical?

### Caveats and Considerations:

- This tool gives only preliminary data. More information is needed before action is taken.
- If managers responding to this checklist are new to dealing with diversity, they may not recognize needs they have.
- This checklist can also be used as a self-assessment by managers by changing the directions and having them rate themselves, either with a plus/minus or on a scale of 1 (not very good) to 5 (very good) on each of the items.

# Sample Focus Group Agenda

1.  Introduction of facilitator and explanation of the general purpose of the focus group sessions, as well as who will see the data.

2.  Self-introduction of participants by name.

3.  Objectives of the group discussion:
    *   Gain employees' perceptions about how the organization is dealing with a diverse work force.
    *   Learn about diversity-related barriers to teamwork, productivity, and motivation.
    *   Hear employees' concerns, ideas, and suggestions about dealing with diversity.

4.  Ground rules of the session:
    *   Confidentiality of sources, with input reported anonymously.
    *   Each person speaks for self.
    *   Every perception is valid; no arguing with perceptions.
    *   One person speaks at a time.
    *   Get permission to tape if desired.

5.  Present questions for discussion, giving participants time to jot down ideas and points. (Questions may be on an overhead transparency, flip chart, and/or handout.)

6.  Facilitate discussion.
    *   Keep participants focused on the questions asked.
    *   Chart comments and responses as stated.
    *   Clarify points and ask for specific examples when vague comments or generalizations are made.
    *   Maintain objectivity and do not enter into the discussion.

7.  Wrap up the discussion, summarizing themes or making a concluding statement that refers back to objectives.

8.  Thank participants and tell them what will happen with data.

# Sample Focus Group Questions

These questions are examples of the kind of discussion "pump primers" you can use to get people talking and to focus their comments on the areas you are investigating.

- What are signs that this organization values a diverse work force?

- What are the obstacles in the way of employees who are different from the mainstream?

- What organizational practices, policies, or norms keep diverse groups from succeeding and/or moving up?

- As a member of a minority group in this organization, how do you feel you are treated?

- What kinds of prejudice or discrimination have you faced, if any?

- What do you wish members of other groups knew about you or your group?

- What do you wish your manager understood about you?

- What do you wish management understood about your group?

- What contributions and behaviors are most valued and rewarded in this organization?

- What do you need to do and/or know to get ahead in this organization?

- What would you like to know and/or learn that could help you succeed here?

- How comfortable, accepted, and valued do you feel in this organization? Why?

- What groups are easiest/hardest for you to work cooperatively with?

- What behaviors of other groups are most difficult for you to deal with or most irritating?

- What do you think the organization could do to get the best from everyone?

# Analyzing Organizational Demographics

|  | Executives Number/ Percent | Managers Number/ Percent | Supervisors Number/ Percent | Staff Number/ Percent |
|---|---|---|---|---|
| **Staff Composition** | | | | |
| Gender: | | | | |
| Male | ___/___ | ___/___ | ___/___ | ___/___ |
| Female | ___/___ | ___/___ | ___/___ | ___/___ |
| Total | ___/___ | ___/___ | ___/___ | ___/___ |
| Ethnicity: | | | | |
| Euro-American | ___/___ | ___/___ | ___/___ | ___/___ |
| African-American | ___/___ | ___/___ | ___/___ | ___/___ |
| Latino | ___/___ | ___/___ | ___/___ | ___/___ |
| Middle Eastern | ___/___ | ___/___ | ___/___ | ___/___ |
| Asian | ___/___ | ___/___ | ___/___ | ___/___ |
| Pacific Islanders | ___/___ | ___/___ | ___/___ | ___/___ |
| Native American | ___/___ | ___/___ | ___/___ | ___/___ |
| Other | ___/___ | ___/___ | ___/___ | ___/___ |
| Total | ___/___ | ___/___ | ___/___ | ___/___ |

**Languages Spoken**

|  | Number | Percent |
|---|---|---|
| Native English speakers | ___ | ___ |
| Fluent, accented-English speakers (strong accent) | ___ | ___ |
| Limited-English speakers (strong accent) | ___ | ___ |
| Non-English speakers | ___ | ___ |
| Bilingual | ___ | ___ |
| Spanish/English | ___ | ___ |
| Tagalog/English | ___ | ___ |
| Japanese/English | ___ | ___ |
| Vietnamese/English | ___ | ___ |
| Chinese (Mandarin)/English | ___ | ___ |
| Chinese (Cantonese)/English | ___ | ___ |
| Arabic/English | ___ | ___ |
| Korean/English | ___ | ___ |
| Armenian/English | ___ | ___ |
| Hebrew/English | ___ | ___ |
| Russian/English | ___ | ___ |
| _____/English | | |

**Personal Data**

|  | Men Number/ Percent | Women Number/ Percent |
|---|---|---|
| Married | ___/___ | ___/___ |
| Single | ___/___ | ___/___ |
| Dual parent | ___/___ | ___/___ |
| Single parent | ___/___ | ___/___ |

# Suggestions for Using *Analyzing Organizational Demographics*

## Objectives:

- Examine organization demographics related to diversity.
- Provide data for analysis and decision making regarding diversity.

## Intended Audience:

- Human resource professionals collecting data for diversity planning.
- Diversity development task forces gathering baseline data.

## Processing the Activity:

- Data collectors gather statistics about each category, compiling information and computing percentages. Data can be gathered through self-report question-naires, personnel records, and/or management observation.
- Data can be analyzed, summarized, and reported to appropriate planning group.

## Questions for Discussion:

- How do organizational statistics compare with those of the work force in the area? Population in the area?
- What surprises or questions are there?
- What do these statistics indicate for the organization in terms of needs, potential opportunities, and possible problems?

## Caveats and Considerations:

- Some individuals may regard information requested as too personal and may balk at the categorization.
- Some individuals will see the categorization as divisive rather than as a first step in remedying deficiencies that may exist.
- Careful explanation of the purposes of this survey and its use in identifying organization needs is required.

# Morale and Work-Group Cohesiveness Observation Checklist

Check those statements that describe your staff most of the time.

_____ Employees of different groups help one another without being asked.

_____ Staff members eat lunch and spend breaks in mixed groups.

_____ Employees talk freely and openly with one another.

_____ There are no cliques or in-group/out-group divisions among staff.

_____ Employees take initiative in solving problems and making suggestions about improvements.

_____ Employees do not blame one another for problems.

_____ Employees freely voice their views to their manager.

_____ Employees are proud to work in this department/unit/division.

_____ There is low absenteeism.

_____ There is low turnover.

_____ There is laughter and good-natured humor in the work group.

_____ No employees are left out of work-group camaraderie.

_____ Employees of different backgrounds work together cooperatively.

_____ There is little friction between staff from different cultures or of different life-styles.

_____ There is seldom petty gossiping or backstabbing.

_____ Employees are willing to help each other out during stressful or demanding times.

_____ The workload is shared equitably by all.

_____ Employees celebrate together.

_____ Employees make an effort to help newcomers become part of the team.

_____ Employees go out of their way to understand employees whose English is limited or accented.

# Suggestions for Using the *Morale and Work-Group Cohesiveness Observation Checklist*

## Objectives:

- Assess work-group morale and cohesiveness.
- Pinpoint obstacles to teamwork.
- Identify employees' irritations, concerns, and problems that may be blocking productivity.

## Intended Audience:

- Managers and supervisors seeking to increase the cohesiveness and morale of their teams.
- Trainees in a management/supervisory development class or managing diversity seminar.
- Members of a diverse work group seeking to strengthen the team.

## Processing the Activity:

- Individuals check those conditions and factors they observe in their work team.
- Groups discuss those items checked and not checked, focusing on strength and weaknesses of the team.
- Items not checked are discussed with regard to their impact on the team.
- Weaknesses are listed and prioritized, and areas for development are targeted.
- Individual managers can target specific areas to begin working on to strengthen their own team.

## Questions for Discussion:

- What strengths and weaknesses are indicated?
- What is at the root of the weaknesses?
- Which issues have highest priority for attention?
- How can these areas be strengthened?
- What can you/we do to begin working on the problems surfaced?

## Caveats and Considerations:

- Managers making observations of their own staffs will tend to lack objectivity. It is helpful to suggest having a few other people in the group or the whole team respond to get a more rounded view.
- Weaknesses indicated need to be investigated further to find out underlying reasons, conditions, and organization systems that may be at the heart.

# Sample Interview Questions for Leaders and Policymakers

1. What have been the biggest benefits of having a multicultural work force? What are the biggest problems and frustrations?

2. With an increasingly diverse work force, what changes do you see in productivity? Interpersonal dynamics? Bottom line (e.g., training dollars spent on education)?

3. What challenges does this present to your organization?

4. What is your organization doing to help your managers meet these challenges? What do they need to learn to do differently?

5. How do you measure and reward your managers in this area?

6. What is your organization doing to enhance the upward mobility of non-dominant-group members? What obstacles prevent this mobility?

7. What processes do you have to identify and develop a diverse pool of talented employees?

8. What does your organization do that shows you value cultural diversity?

9. What is your organization doing to accommodate differences in values, norms, and mores?

10. What made you decide to invest your organization's resources (time, energy, money) in making diversity development a priority? What results have you seen?

11. What organizational systems, practices, and policies present obstacles to fully developing and utilizing your diverse work force?

12. If your organization does nothing to address the cultural diversity issue, what do you predict will happen?

# Sample Interview Questions for Non-Dominant-Culture Employees

1. What do you like about the culture of this organization?

2. What do you find difficult about it?

3. What did you expect to find when you came to work here? What was your biggest surprise? Biggest joy? Biggest disappointment?

4. What kinds of experiences made you feel welcome in this organization? Unwelcome? What did you do to help the situation?

5. What is your professional goal? What do you hope to achieve here?

6. How has this organization helped you toward your goal? How could it help more?

7. Have you ever felt it was a mistake to come to work here? If so, what made you feel this way?

8. How have you been treated by bosses and co-workers (both good and bad news)?

9. How do you get along with people of other groups in the workplace?

10. On a scale of 1 to 10, how much do you feel a part of the organization? What needs to happen to make you feel more a part of it?

11. What is the most important thing the organization can do to help you adjust? What can you do?

# Sample Interview Questions for Dominant-Culture Employees

1. What have been the biggest changes in this organization the past few years?

2. What have been the biggest benefits of being part of a multicultural work force? What are the biggest problems and frustrations?

3. How does diversity in the work force impact you? Your work group? This organization?

4. What has been the biggest "culture shock" for you in working with diverse groups?

5. What kinds of experiences make you feel comfortable with employees from different groups? Uncomfortable? What did you do to help the situation?

6. How have you been treated by employees of diverse groups?

7. What is the most important thing your organization can do to help non-dominant-group members adapt to this organization?

8. What is the most important thing these employees can do to help themselves adapt?

# Neutralizing the Application Process Checklist

Answer each of the questions below by putting a check in the column that most accurately reflects the behavior of you or your organization.

| Questions | Rarely | Sometimes | Often |
|---|---|---|---|
| 1. All applicants are given the same information and get their questions answered. | ___ | ___ | ___ |
| 2. When language problems exist, our organization finds a way around them through the use of pictures, interpreters, or the like. | ___ | ___ | ___ |
| 3. Every interviewee for a particular job is asked the same questions. While interview style may change due to personal and cultural differences, the interview process is standard. | ___ | ___ | ___ |
| 4. Interviewers avoid prejudging applicants based on appearance. | ___ | ___ | ___ |
| 5. Interviewers don't jumpt to conclusions about someone's ability to do the job based on race, gender, age, ethnicity, or physical ability. | ___ | ___ | ___ |
| 6. Interviewers and managers recognize and compensate for their own hiring preferences. | ___ | ___ | ___ |
| 7. Applicants are interviewed by a diverse team. | ___ | ___ | ___ |
| 8. There is a male/female mix on the interview team. | ___ | ___ | ___ |
| 9. Interviewers are aware of cultural "hot spots" and avoid issues that may offend applicants. | ___ | ___ | ___ |
| 10. Written application questions have been tested for cultural bias and ease of understanding. | ___ | ___ | ___ |

# Suggestions for Using the *Neutralizing the Application Process Checklist*

## Objectives:

- Gain a sense of the openness and neutrality of your organization's application process for new hires.
- Get feedback from those in positions to hire, or recent new hires.
- Educate those in a position to bring new people on board.

## Intended Audience:

- HR professional in charge of recruiting and hiring or in charge of educating managers about hiring.
- Managers who do their own hiring.
- Work teams who interview and pick new hires.
- Vice president in charge of HR who wants to raise the issue at top levels of the organization.

## Processing the Activity:

- Distribute the questionnaire to those charged with the task of interviewing and hiring new employees. This can be given in a workshop setting or to individuals one-on-one.
- Ask them to respond by putting a check in the appropriate column. Then score the checklist.
- Whether in a workshop setting or discussed one-on-one, ask respondent to look at one- and two-point answers.

## Questions for Discussion:

- What do the data from this questionnaire indicate about your application process?
- Where can you or your interview team pat yourselves on the back for creating an open and neutral environment?
- What do you need to still do to make it more so?

## Caveats and Considerations:

- If an HR vice president gives this to one manager, he or she may suggest that the whole interview team look it over and discuss it before the next interview.
- This would be a good tool to give to recent new hires for feedback. That information could be distributed to the appropriate sources.

# Recruitment and Retention Strategies of Vons Groceries (A Chain of Southern California Supermarkets)

| Group | Recruitment Strategies |
|---|---|
| Minorities | Early school links |
| | Explain opportunities |
| | Identified career paths |
| | Image enhancement |
| | Role models |
| | Cultural awareness |
| Homemakers | Increased flexibility |
| | Child-care considerations |
| | School-term-only jobs |
| | Image enhancement |
| | Wage/benefit information |
| Retirees | Increased flexibility |
| | Image enhancement |
| | Role models |
| | Recruitment targets |
| | Wage/benefit information |
| | Part-time shifts |
| Students | Increased flexibility |
| | School-term-only jobs |
| | Image enhancement |
| | Wage/benefit information |
| | OJT programs |
| | Identified career paths |
| Mentally/ physically challenged | Agency contacts |
| | Explain opportunities |
| | Role models |
| | OJT programs |
| | Job content-flexibility |
| **Retention Strategies** | Employee orientation |
| | Service training |
| | Management training |
| | Literacy training |
| | Employee association |
| | Service awards |
| | Retention bonuses |

# Recognizing Values Differences in Your Hiring and Promotion Process

| Mainstream America | Most Other Cultures | Impact |
|---|---|---|
| 1. Work and obligation to the job are a high priority for many. | Primary obligation is to family and friends. | This values difference often causes American managers to question the loyalty and commitment that diverse employees have toward the company, as well as their motivation to do the job. |
| 2. An organization has the right to terminate an employee. An employee has the right to leave a company for a variety of reasons. | Employment is for one's lifetime. | If an employee from another culture is terminated for not meeting performance standards, it may disgrace the employee. In addition to loss of face for the individual, there is the possibility that members of the same group will interpret termination as an affront. It could demoralize and affect group commitment and loyalty. The expectation of lifetime employment may make some managers gun-shy when they consider hiring someone from a diverse background. |
| 3. There is a strong drive for personal achievement. | Personal ambition is frowned upon. | People who frown on personal ambition and who place group loyalty before personal reward may be perceived as lazy or unmotivated. Individuals from cultures where "tooting your own horn" is discouraged may not feel it is appropriate to seek promotion or even mention an interest in doing so. Managers will need to keep a special lookout for these "diamonds in the rough" and encourage them to take advantage of developmental activities, or sign up for promotional exams. |
| 4. Competition is a valued way of stimulating performance. | Competition upsets balance and harmony. | People from immigrant cultures may not indicate interest in promoting or setting themselves apart from the crowd because loyalty to the group and a harmonious environment are more important. The danger here for the American manager is the false assumption that the person isn't motivated to do an excellent job and that he isn't aggressive or assertive enough to get the job done. |
| 5. Loyalty is to the organization. | Loyalty is to individuals such as bosses or informal group leaders. | Employees from cultures that emphasize personal loyalty may see promotion as an act of disloyalty and lack of gratitude toward one's boss. Organizations need to understand the strong pull of boss and peer group loyalty when offering promotions and understand why this opportunity might not be received enthusiastically. |

# Creative Cultural Networking Checklist

Put a check by any statements that reflect what you are currently doing.

_____  1. I belong to professional or social group where the membership is very diverse.

_____  2. I consciously attend group functions where I am an outsider, where I don't know many people, and where some of them are of a different group (e.g., gender, ethnicity, race, or religion).

_____  3. I create collegial relationships, friendships, or arrangements at work with people who are different from me.

_____  4. At meetings, functions, or professional conferences, I make it my business to expand my contacts with people from diverse groups.

_____  5. I attend various cultural support groups such as the Black Employees' Association at work, even though by background I am not a member of those networking groups.

_____  6. I attend community functions, lectures, art exhibits, or holidays that celebrate diverse cultures.

_____  7. I join civic groups apart from work where I have a chance to broaden my contacts.

_____  8. I have hosted a networking party where I invited people from diverse backgrounds and asked them all to invite a friend or colleague.

_____  9. I keep nurturing the relationships I have already developed so that my base of contacts grows.

_____  10. I have joined an organization or currently subscribe to a publication whose top priority is cultural diversity.


**Directions for scoring:** Count your checks. The more you have, the more productively you create your cultural network. Our suggestion is that you target one or two of these specific items as a beginning point toward expanding your cultural network.

1. One thing I will do to more creatively develop my diversity network is _____ and I will do so by (date) _____ .

2. One thing I'm already doing well but could improve on a little is _____. I plan to capitalize on this networking technique by doing the following: _____.

# Suggestions for Using the *Creative Cultural Networking Checklist*

### Objectives:

- Offer suggestions about various places to expand contacts and gain greater access to pluralistic work force.
- Assess current outreach efforts.

### Intended Audience:

- Human resource professional or manager in charge of hiring and promoting.
- Affirmative action officers in charge of hiring and promoting.
- External consultants specializing in diversity management who want to expand their network.

### Processing the Activity:

- This self-assessment tool is primarily designed for those whose responsibility it is to expand the mix of employees at all levels of the organization through recruiting and promotion efforts. A single individual can take this assessment, see the results, and use it as a blueprint for greater outreach.
- If there is a companywide or divisionwide effort to expand the employee mix, this could be useful in a workshop setting to determine an organization-wide strategy.
- Have participants check the response they are engaged in. See what activities are not being covered by the group; then determine what efforts need to be made.
- The facilitator can take each item, one at a time, and see who is doing what. Areas ripe for exploration will emerge in the discussion.

### Questions for Discussion:

- How many of you are involved in item number _____?
- What have been your results?
- What makes this work well?
- Are there things that might make this strategy more effective?
- Where should we put our energy as a group?
- Let's define commitment more specifically. Where are you willing to put your energy?

### Caveats and Considerations:

- This can be very effective as a tool for individuals. Vice presidents of HR may want to share it with appropriate people on an as-needed basis.

# Cultural Awareness Questionnaire
# (How Culturally Knowledgeable Are You?)

Directions: Please respond to each of the questions below with a check in the appropriate column.

|  | Yes | No |
|---|---|---|
| 1. I know that different cultural values and behaviors may influence my perceptions of a person's competence, confidence, and social graces. | ____ | ____ |
| 2. I have ways of being less direct in asking questions of someone from Mexico or the Middle East in order to get information and help the interviewee feel at ease. | ____ | ____ |
| 3. In cultures where the group is more important than the individual, I have ways to gain information about a person's performance by focusing on group goals and the individual's part in them. | ____ | ____ |
| 4. Regarding introductions, I appropriately use first names and surnames. | ____ | ____ |
| 5. I understand that not making eye contact is often a way of showing respect, not a lack of assertiveness. | ____ | ____ |
| 6. I know when to use both sturdy and soft handshakes, depending on the culture. | ____ | ____ |
| 7. I understand that vagueness in answering a question is often culturally correct. | ____ | ____ |
| 8. I conduct the interview formally because the informality of American culture can be intimidating for an interviewee whose comfort comes partially from a hierarchical structure. | ____ | ____ |
| 9. I am conscious of the fact that standing very close to someone is appropriate in Middle Eastern culture. | ____ | ____ |
| 10. I realize that the loudness or softness with which people talk is often cultural. | ____ | ____ |

# Scoring the *Cultural Awareness Questionnaire*

The more *yes* answers you have, the more culturally aware you are. If any of the cultural behaviors embedded in these 10 questions surprised you, start paying attention to them as you see them in the work arena. Look at your *no* answers. Have you ever come across these behaviors? If so, can you remember your responses or reactions? In order not to have any of these behaviors impede your selection of new personnel, look at how some of them might be your own cultural barriers. Then respond to the questions below.

**To Overcome Your Own Cultural Barriers in Interviewing:**

1.  Which of these behaviors are most troublesome for you?

_____

_____

_____

2.  How do you interpret these behaviors? What is the reason they are problematic?

_____

_____

_____

3.  What are you willing to do, or how are you willing to see things differently, in order to make sure this behavior does not negatively impact the interviewing you do?

_____

_____

_____

## Suggestions for Using the *Cultural Awareness Questionnaire*

### Objectives:

- Educate interviewers about cultural norms that may impact how they treat and view a potential employee.
- Provide an assessment tool that increases cultural and self-awareness.

### Intended Audience:

- HR professionals or affirmative action officers in charge of interviewing and hiring or in charge of educating managers about interviewing and hiring.
- Managers who do their own interviewing.
- Work teams who interview and pick new hires.
- Vice president in charge of HR who wants to educate and sensitize the executive staff.

### Processing the Activity:

- This tool can be used for groups being educated about cultural differences. It can also be given to managers of other individuals who need cultural awareness because they interview, hire, or promote.
- If used with a group, pass it out to participants, have them discuss in pairs or small groups.
- Discuss questions in whole group. Be sure that the last three questions, on overcoming culture barriers, are discussed as well.

### Questions for Discussion:

- What cultural behaviors or values surprised you?
- Which of these behaviors are most troublesome for you?
- How do you interpret these behaviors? What makes them problematic?
- What changes are you willing to make in your own interviewing?

### Caveats and Considerations:

- HR professionals or affirmative action officers can give this to managers of people who need it and discuss it one-on-one. It can be a useful coaching/teaching tool.
- You can make this tool more culturally specific if you are trying to educate your staff to deal more effectively with a particular consumer or employee base.

# Five Ways to Ask Questions
## (That Set Up Any Candidate for Success)

| Question-Asking Style | Advantage | Disadvantage |
|---|---|---|
| 1. Open-ended questions | Designed to explore options or design possibilities. Good at the beginning of discussion process. In passive languages, easy to frame questions. | Time consuming; not designed to give specific information so getting to concrete answers can be a lengthy process. |
| 2. Closed-ended questions | Narrows responses; gets very concrete. | Not designed to let you see the creativity or ability to suggest options that may be a strength in a candidate's thinking. |
| 3. Speculative questions | Designed to encourage vision and reflect on possibilities that don't exist or may seem unlikely; can really showcase creative thinkers. | Some groups, particularly the Japanese, find this style unfathomable—not in their thinking style to deal with questions of this nature. |
| 4. "Tell me . . . ." | Because these two words are a question disguised as a statement, it feels less intrusive. It will open people up who may not like to be questioned. | If people are not concise, they can ramble and go off on a tangent. |
| 5. "Describe . . . ." | Like "Tell me . . . ," this also solicits information without seeming intrusive. It will create more openness and less defensiveness. | This also can be time-consuming if people ramble or go off on a tangent. |

# Sample Interview Questions

1. What makes this job opening interesting to you?

2. Tell me (or us) why you want to work for this company.

3. What things mean the most to you in any job? In what order of importance?

4. Describe the position as you understand the job. Talk about your experiences in these areas.

5. What qualifications would you look for in a candidate for this job if you were doing the hiring? What attributes do you think would be most essential to job success in this position?

6. How would you distinguish an outstanding employee from a typical one in any job?

7. What have you learned in your past schooling and training that you think would be helpful in the job you are currently applying for?

8. What has your group accomplished in your past position that you feel would be indicative of successful performance in this job? What did your group find most difficult?

9. What did you enjoy most about your previous jobs, co-workers, supervisors, departments, companies, and industries?

10. How did you happen to choose the jobs you have held?

11. Let me describe a situation that we are dealing with in this unit. What are your suggestions for dealing with it?

12. What has your past experience been in dealing with cliques? What has been the biggest impediment to a cohesive work team in your past jobs? How would you change that if you found the same circumstances here?

In the blanks below, rephrase your own questions to be more culturally sensitive.

1. _____

2. _____

3. _____

4. _____

5. _____

# Interviewing Assumptions and Biases

Directions: Answer the following five questions. The more candid you are, the more helpful this information will be.

1. What behaviors do I currently expect to look for from someone I interview or hire? Consider the following areas specifically:

   • Language skills/usage

   _____

   _____

   • Communication style (verbal and nonverbal)

   _____

   _____

   _____

   • Etiquette (involves social norms such as handshakes, how people are introduced, and distance between people)

   _____

   _____

   • Social values (egalitarianism vs. hierarchical structure)

   _____

   _____

   _____

2. What assumptions do I make about potential interviewees and their competence when I see different behaviors than I want or am used to?

   • Language:

   _____

   _____

   _____

   • Communication:

   _____

   _____

   _____

# Interviewing Assumptions and Biases (concluded)

- Etiquette:
  _____

  _____

  _____

- Values:
  _____

  _____

  _____

**3.** What differences are easy for me to handle?

_____

_____

_____

**4.** What differences are a problem?

_____

_____

_____

**5.** What does this suggest I need to do differently to be more sensitive when I interview people of color, the differently abled, older workers, or those with a different affectional orientation?

_____

_____

_____

## Suggestions for Using *Interviewing Assumptions and Biases*

### Objectives:

- Identify biases or assumptions in areas of language, communication, style, etiquette, and social values that impact the interviewing and selection process.
- Determine where biases can sabotage recruitment efforts.

### Intended Audience:

- HR professional or affirmative action officer in charge of recruiting.
- Manager in charge of recruiting.
- Work team that hires its own team members.
- Vice president of HR who wants to coach particular managers.

### Processing the Activity:

- This can be used with teams who hire their co-workers or by HR professionals who want to coach a manager one-on-one. In either case, it needs to be filled out first.
- If a team uses this to broaden its awareness of biases, a facilitator would ask team members to share in pairs first, then discuss as a whole group.
- A group discussion would follow.

### Questions for Discussion:

- Use the five questions in the questionnaire to guide your discussion, focusing on four areas: (1) language, (2) communication style, (3) etiquette, and (4) social values.
- All five questions are important, but ultimately, numbers 4 and 5 need to be discussed fully: What differences are a problem? What does this mean I (we) need to do differently?

### Caveats and Considerations:

- Like all the tools in this chapter, this can be used with a group, but it can also be very helpful in coaching managers one-on-one.

# Evaluating the Trade-Offs of the Male and Female Management Prototypes

Directions: List the gains and losses you see in your organization from perceived male and female management styles.

**Male**

| Prototype | Gains | Losses |
|---|---|---|
| Leading by command and control | | |
| Enhancing rewards for services rendered | | |
| Reliance on positional power | | |
| Following a hierarchical quasi-military structure | | |
| Action orientation | | |
| Analytical thinking and linear problem solving | | |

**Female**

| Prototype | Gains | Losses |
|---|---|---|
| Sharing power and information | | |
| Enhancing self-worth of others | | |
| Encouraging participation | | |
| Getting others excited about their work | | |

## Suggestions for Using *Evaluating Trade-Offs of the Male and Female Management Prototypes*

### Objectives:

- Consider what the traditional male and female models of leadership give to and take from your organization.

### Intended Audience:

- Executive or midmanagement staffs that want to address the issue of what qualities are rewarded and promoted.
- Executive or midmanagement staffs that want to open up the system and make a commitment to more diverse representation at the top.

### Processing the Activity:

- Have individual participants fill out the worksheet first.
- Then have a group discussion about the gains and losses derived from each of the various characteristics.

### Questions for Discussion:

- What do these stereotypically male and female characteristics contribute to the organization?
- What do we reward around here?
- What is it costing us?
- How can we open up the system?
- What management skills are missing from this list that we need to reward?
- How can we ensure a broadening of the skills we reward and more representation from all segments of society?

### Caveats and Considerations:

- Participants may react to the issue of *male* and *female*. They'll say "All males don't . . ." and "all females don't . . . ." Setting up the activity by citing the studies from which the data came, and by acknowledging that they do not refer to "all males" or "all females" can help diffuse resistance. Explain that these are generalizations but that there is some reason they exist. Your purpose is not to label or pigeonhole either gender, but rather to open up the system.

# Valued Management Traits

I.  List the 10 most important traits your company looks for in someone it promotes to a management position:

_____     _____

_____     _____

_____     _____

_____     _____

_____     _____

1.  Put a check by each trait that describes you.

2.  Put an *X* by each characteristic that is valued by the dominant American business culture.

3.  What is the flip side of each of these characteristics?

4.  Are any of these traits more difficult for a woman? Person of color? The differently skilled? Someone of a different affectional orientation?

II. List traits that you see frequently in other groups on the job that "hold them back."

_____     _____

_____     _____

_____     _____

_____     _____

1.  What are some advantages to these traits?

2.  If you were to coach someone of another group for a management position, how would you help that person with traits that you perceive hold him or her back?

# Suggestions for Using *Valued Management Traits*

**Objectives:**

- Identify management traits that are rewarded and promoted in your organization.
- See how similar you and other managers or executives are to that management model.
- Consider how difficult it might be for someone from the nondominant culture to succeed and be promoted in your organization.
- Get a sense that other cultures have traits we can learn from.

**Intended Audience:**

- Facilitator, consultant, or HR professional working with a middle management group to help look at opening their promotion process.
- Affirmative action officer or vice president of HR who wants to help an executive staff understand current promotability with an eye toward opening up the system.

**Processing the Activity:**

- Ask participants to fill out the worksheet. When working with an executive staff, discuss responses among the whole group. For a middle management group, break up into small groups first, then process with the entire group.
- Chart the list of characteristics on an easel in front of the group. Put checks by those characteristics.

**Questions for Discussion:**

- Discuss each of the other questions with the biggest focus on What are we promoting? How does this model of promotability hold a diverse candidate back? What can we do about it?

**Caveats and Considerations:**

- Do not even begin the analyses of valued management traits unless you are willing to do something about broadening the criteria. Looking at the issue will raise expectations, but doing nothing will create cynicism and hopelessness.

# What Does Your Company Do to Increase Promotions of Its Diverse Employees?

Directions: With your organization in mind, respond to the following questions by putting a check in the appropriate column.

| Questions | Yes | No |
|---|---|---|
| 1. Top management utilizes formal systems to meet with and encourage top talent from diverse backgrounds. | ___ | ___ |
| 2. Teaching potential "stars" the rules is a top priority. | ___ | ___ |
| 3. A balanced life is compatible with the demanding work load of those who move up. | ___ | ___ |
| 4. Our company is attractive to diverse employees because we are flexible enough to accommodate differences. | ___ | ___ |
| 5. Our company models change by welcoming diversity at all levels of the organization. | ___ | ___ |
| 6. A formal mentoring system exists to nurture top talent. | ___ | ___ |
| 7. The golf course is the best place to tap into the informal pipeline. | ___ | ___ |
| 8. Taking parental leave is possible but frowned upon. | ___ | ___ |
| 9. Our organization can sell itself to diverse employees by pointing out that 25 percent of top management are currently women and people of color. | ___ | ___ |
| 10. Involvement in change is pushed to the lowest level of the organization. | ___ | ___ |
| 11. Top management seeks advice from and contact with employees from all backgrounds. | ___ | ___ |
| 12. Our organization reaches out to and is knowledgeable about the population it serves. | ___ | ___ |
| 13. A reward structure exists to accommodate the different employee motivations. | ___ | ___ |
| 14. Our company has an excellent reputation in attracting top talent because of our child- and elder-care policies. | ___ | ___ |
| 15. Many of our systems are different today than they were one year ago. | ___ | ___ |

**Scoring:** Items number 7 and 8 are *no* answers and all the rest should be *yes* if your organization promotes advancement of diverse individuals. Here are the concepts being measured:

Items 1, 6, 11 *Building connections:* Helps employees develop and maintain relationships that are sturdy and enhancing at all levels of the organization.

Items 2, 7, 12: *Political savvy:* Helps employees make use of the informal organization and pick up the unstated clues.

Items 3, 8, 13: *Dealing with multiple motivations:* Demonstrates a willingness to be flexible with today's work force, realizing that different employees are motivated by different things.

Items 4, 9, 14: *Positioning:* Indicates the organization's ability to make itself attractive by presenting outcomes in a value base employees respect and respond to.

Items 5, 10, 15: *Mastering change:* Attests to an organization's openness to new people, ideas, and systems.

## Suggestions for Using *What Does Your Company Do to Increase Promotions of Its Diverse Employees?*

**Objectives:**

* Assess your organization's openness to promoting diverse employees.

**Intended Audience:**

* Executive-level staff to see how open they perceive the organization to be and where they can be more so.
* Middle management to give executive staff feedback about openness as they see it.

**Processing the Activity:**

* Have each participant take and score the questionnaire.
* In executive staff, discuss as a whole group; for midlevel management, break into small groups first.
* Collate results from midlevel management and feed upward.

**Questions for Discussion:**

* What item number and category do you see as this organization's greatest strength in opening up the system?
* Its greatest weakness?
* What, according to the data, needs to be done in order to expand the promotional system?

**Caveats and Considerations:**

* Don't give this to midlevel managers to send feedback upward if there won't be any movement. The disenchantment and disappointment will be too costly.

# Norms: The Unwritten Rules of This Organization

**Dress**
What is the organizational uniform? How do people dress? Who wears suits? At what level are jackets required? Do women wear pants?

| | Men | Women |
|---|---|---|
| Top executives | | |
| Senior management | | |
| Middle management | | |
| Supervisors | | |
| First-line staff | | |
| Other | | |

**Communicating and Addressing**
How are people addressed? (First name, title, etc.) How are people contacted? (Phone call, memo, appointment)

| | Men | Women |
|---|---|---|
| Top executives | | |
| Senior management | | |
| Middle management | | |
| Supervisors | | |
| First-line staff | | |
| Other | | |

**Employee Gatherings/Interacting**
Who interacts? Who invites whom? How much time is spent? Is promptness valued/expected?

| | Format (Where, When, Interaction) | Participants (Who, Roles) |
|---|---|---|
| Meetings | | |
| Breaks | | |
| Lunch | | |
| After work | | |

## Suggestions for Using *Norms: The Unwritten Rules of This Organization*

**Objectives:**

- Help potential managers learn the unwritten rules of behavior in your company.

**Intended Audience:**

- Coaches working with potential promotees so they can teach them the "rules."

**Processing the Activity:**

- One-on-one discussion between coach and promotee.

**Questions for Discussion:**

- Whatever is on the worksheet and whatever other norms the coach suggests are important.

**Caveats and Considerations:**

- It is possible for a trainer to bring coaches together and use a seminar format to collectively determine what the norms are so that all coaches in a given organization teach and reinforce the same ones.

# Coaching for Promotion

As a unit manager in systems planning, Maryann Ransom, a lesbian, has just come to work for you. She has a B.A. from a state university and graduated in the top third of the class. Her first job out of business school was as a management trainee at Merck, where she received excellent training in basic supervisory skills and computer programming. Working with you, her job duties will involve budget planning and analysis, project management, and supervision of a small group of data processors. References indicate good peer relationships, initiative, creativity, and great promise. Maryann is also an active member of the Gay and Lesbian Rights Association.

The quality of her work has been excellent; however, she has had little experience in some key areas required for the new job such as personnel relations, EEOC and affirmative action guidelines, and hiring and interviewing skills.

1. What would you do to help groom Maryann for promotion?

2. How would you coach her to develop the skills and experiences necessary to move up in the organization?

3. List 10 steps you would take or suggest to enhance Maryann's development and career success.

# Suggestions for Using *Coaching for Promotion*

**Objectives:**

- Determine whether people are coached differently because of ethnicity, race, gender, or other aspects of background.
- Detect any biases in who is promoted.

**Intended Audience:**

- Facilitator, consultant, HR professional, or trainer who is charged with the task of helping mid- and upper-level management see if there is any bias in how people are coached.

**Processing the Activity:**

- Use the worksheet, changing only the name and background of the person and keeping the criteria the same.
- Divide people into small groups. Have them discuss coaching strategy and then report back to entire group about their strategy. Write strategies on chart paper.

**Questions for Discussion:**

After each group reports its coaching strategy, discuss what differences emerge based on background.

- What differences in coaching exist? Depending on what factors? How can they be minimized?

**Caveats and Considerations:**

- Make certain that the different employee populations in your geographic area are represented.
- Don't let participants know that candidate names are different but qualities are the same.

# Impact of Values on Career Expectations and Performance

| Point of Contact | Mainstream Culture | Other Cultures |
|---|---|---|
| Interview | I need to showcase my experience, skills, and talents. | My track record and seniority speak for themselves. I need to establish a relationship and get comfortable with the other person first. |
| Performance review | I need feedback so I can do a better job. | Criticism could cause me to lose face and feel shame. |
| Meetings | Making suggestions and actively participating show I am motivated and take the initiative. | Contributing my ideas, asking questions, voicing complaints, or making suggestions look like I am showing off and may make my boss lose face. Besides, ideas and suggestions need to come from the leader. |
| Socializing/networking | I'm going to these events because you never know who will be there. The visibility can't hurt my career. | I will go to this event because my boss asked me to and I wouldn't let her down. |
| Mentoring | I'd like the CEO to be my mentor because he has the clout in this organization. If he's in my corner, it will certainly help. | I like my boss, Miss Shirley. She is a very nice person who treats me with respect. |
| Self-promotion | Expected and rewarded; to paraphrase American Express, "Don't expect a promotion without it." | Very difficult for other cultures; it would be embarrassing and a violation of some of the most sacrosanct norms to toot your own horn. |
| Forming alliances | Pragmatic in the dominant culture; people and organizations are political. This is a survival skill. | Inclusion in the group and relationships are critical. They are formed because of personal loyalty and affection, not because of position in the organization. |
| Social skills; ice breaking; establishing rapport | The dominant culture is short on social lubrication, long on getting right to the point. Self-introduction is accepted and sometimes expected. | This skill could be a natural ally for most other cultures where far more time is invested in relationships. Formal introductions are expected. Individuals may be reluctant to establish relationships outside of their own group. |
| Giving and getting feedback | Needed and expected skills for one's growth; "If you don't give me feedback, how can I know what I need to do differently or better?" Done in the good old American way—directly. Separation of the behavior from the worth of a person makes it more objective and less personal. | This is very delicate in other cultures. Loss of face warrants shame. People have left jobs because of negative feedback and the perception of disgrace. Feedback is often taken personally and seen as a personal affront. |
| Tapping the grapevine | Skeptical of informal communication. There is a tendency to believe what is in print and official. | Those out of power generally make the greatest use of the grapevine and are often skeptical of official information channels. |
| Scheduling/goal setting | Task and time consciousness, coupled with linear thinking and planning matter. Anything can be done or accomplished if the individual works hard enough. Each person is responsible for his/her own success or failure. | Time is relative and the accomplishment of tasks depends on more than the individual alone. Other priorities often change schedules and plans. Fate and the will of God play a part. |

# Career Development Model

1. **Top down:** Build career development through all the systems. Some examples are:

   - Performance review.

   - Recruitment/hiring/promotion.

   - Accountability.

   - Training.

2. **Bottom up:** Conduct skill training for managers and employees in various diversity-related areas. Some examples are:

**Managers:**

   - Giving performance reviews in culturally sensitive ways.

   - Handling intercultural conflict.

   - Running effective meetings in a diverse environment.

   - Conducting interviews in culturally appropriate ways.

   - Building effective multicultural work teams.

   - Recognizing cultural biases in making promotions.

   - Expanding the list of valued management characteristics.

**Employees:**

   - Building connections.

   - Becoming politically savvy.

   - Learning to position ideas effectively.

   - Managing and becoming comfortable with change.

   - Becoming comfortably assertive.

   - Gaining self-promotion skills.

# Analyzing Your Organization's Work-Force Trends

**Population Demographics**

1.  What is the projected breakdown of the community's population in 5 and 10 years in such areas as age, ethnicity, gender, and native language?

2.  What is the projected breakdown of the local work force in 5 and 10 years by age, ethnicity, and gender?

3.  What are the statistics regarding education level of the work force in 5 and 10 years by gender and ethnicity?

4.  What different needs will these workers bring? How will they impact the organization?

**Organizational Skills Needs**

1.  What is the projected number of new workers needed by your organization in 5 and 10 years by skill level such as unskilled, semiskilled, managerial, professional, and/or by type of work such as assembly line, clerical, data entry, and so on?

2.  What is the projected gain or loss of employees by your organization in 5 and 10 years by department or function such as manufacturing, accounting, data processing, personnel, sales, marketing, and customer relations?

3.  What will be the skill requirements of employees in 5 and 10 years, for example, English literacy or computer literacy?

**Training and Development Needs**

1.  What tools do we need to develop to assess individual skill levels and job requirements?

2.  What basic and job-specific skills will need to be taught to employees?

3.  What managerial skills will need to be taught to those in supervisory and management roles?

# Affirmative Action, Valuing Differences, and Managing Diversity Compared

| Affirmative Action | Valuing Differences | Managing Diversity |
|---|---|---|
| *Quantitative:* Emphasizes achieving equality of opportunity in the work environment through the changing of organizational demographics. Monitored by statistical reports and analysis. | *Qualitative:* Emphasizes the appreciation of differences and creating an environment in which everyone feels valued and accepted. Monitored by organizational surveys focused on attitudes and perceptions. | *Behavioral:* Emphasizes the building of specific skills and creating policies which get the best from every employee. Monitored by progress toward achieving goals and objectives. |
| *Legally driven:* Written plans and statistical goals for specific group are utilized. Reports are mandated by EEO laws and consent decrees. | *Ethically driven:* Moral and ethical imperatives drive this culture change. | *Strategically driven:* Behaviors and policies are seen as contributing to organizational goals and objectives such as profit and productivity and are tied to reward and results. |
| *Remedial:* Specific target groups benefit as past wrongs are remedied. Previously excluded groups have an advantage. | *Idealistic:* Everyone benefits. Everyone feels valued and accepted in an inclusive environment. | *Pragmatic:* The organization benefits; morale, profit, and productivity increase. |
| *Assimilation model:* Assumes that groups brought into system will adapt to existing organizational norms. | *Diversity model:* Assumes that groups will retain their own characteristics and shape the organization as well as be shaped by it, creating a common set of values. | *Synergy model:* Assumes that diverse groups will create new ways of working together effectively in a pluralistic environment. |
| *Opens doors in the organization:* Affects hiring and promotion decisions. | *Opens attitudes, minds, and the culture:* Affects attitudes of employees. | *Opens the system:* Affects managerial practices and policies. |
| *Resistance due to* perceived limits to autonomy in decision making and perceived fears of reverse discrimination. | *Resistance due to* fear of change, discomfort with differences, and desire for return to "good old days." | *Resistance due to* denial of demographic realities, the need for alternative approaches, and/or benefits associated with change; and the difficulty in learning new skills, altering existing systems, and/or finding time to work toward synergistic solutions. |

# How Does Your Organization Measure Up?

Directions: Check off each statement on the list below that describes your organization or department.

**Affirmative action is effective when:**

_____ There is a good faith effort to recruit, hire, train, and promote qualified employees from underrepresented groups.

_____ There is a diverse staff at all levels.

_____ The composition of management staff reflects the composition of the work force in general.

_____ Internal networking surfaces qualified candidates who are from diverse groups.

_____ Mechanisms exist to identify and mentor diverse employees who show promotional potential.

_____ Managers recognize it as their responsibility to make progress in building teams that reflect the composition of the work force.

_____ There are few gripes about preferential treatment and reverse discrimination.

_____ Diverse individuals who are promoted are accepted in their new positions by the rest of staff.

_____ Managers' pay raises are tied to acheiving affirmative action goals.

**Differences are valued when:**

_____ Turnover among all groups is relatively proportionate.

_____ Employees form friendships across racial, cultural, life-style, and gender lines.

_____ Employees talk openly about differences in backgrounds, values, and needs.

_____ No group in the organization is the target of ridicule, jokes, or slurs.

_____ Individuals feel comfortable being themselves at work.

_____ It would not be surprising to employees if the next CEO is not a Euro-American, able-bodied man.

**Diversity is being managed effectively when:**

_____ Leave, absentee, and holiday policies are flexible enough to suit everyone.

_____ Cultural conflicts are resolved and not allowed to fester/escalate.

_____ Employees of all backgrounds feel free to give input and make requests to management.

_____ Diverse employees take advantage of career enhancement opportunities.

_____ Diverse teams work cooperatively and harmoniously.

_____ Productivity of diverse teams is high.

_____ Managers get commitment and cooperation from their diverse staffs.

_____ Organizational procedures such as performance review and career development have been restructured to suit the diverse needs of employees.

_____ There is diverse staff at all levels.

## Suggestions for Using *How Does Your Organization Measure Up?*

**Objectives:**

- Assess your organization's effectiveness with regard to affirmative action, valuing differences, and managing diversity.
- Pinpoint diversity-related issues that need attention.
- Give feedback to executive management and human resource departments regarding aspects of diversity development.

**Intended Audience:**

- Managers, supervisors, and other staff members wanting to give feedback to human resource departments and executive management.
- Executives setting strategic planning goals.

**Processing the Activity:**

- Individuals respond by checking those statements that describe their organizations or departments.
- Responses are tabulated and data are presented to executive management and/or human resource professionals in charge of dealing with diversity issues.
- Executive and/or human resource staff analyze data and identify obstacles to capitalizing on diversity within the organization; they then plan ways to address these barriers.

**Caveats and Considerations:**

- These issues can provoke emotional and heated responses. This assessment activity can best be managed in small groups where venting can take place safely.
- Executives and/or human resource professionals on the receiving end of this feedback may react defensively. Help them to see the responses as valid perceptions of respondees so they can use it constructively.
- This assessment can also be used by affirmative action and human resource professionals in planning and training.

# Section III

## TRANSPARENCY MASTERS

# WORKFORCE TRENDS

✔ Increase in women

✔ Increase in people of color

✔ Increase in immigrants

✔ Aging

✔ Rise in education and skill requirements

# WORKFORCE DIVERSITY

## BUSINESS IMPERATIVE AND COMPETITIVE EDGE

- Better return on the investment in human capital

- Attracting and retaining the best and the brightest

- Innovation through increased creativity

- Ability to capitalize on a diverse market

- Increased adaptability that ensures survival

# PRIMARY AND SECONDARY DIMENSIONS OF DIVERSITY

## PRIMARY

- ✔ Age
- ✔ Ethnicity
- ✔ Gender
- ✔ Physical Ability
- ✔ Race
- ✔ Sexual/Affectional Orientation

## SECONDARY

- ✔ Educational Background
- ✔ Geographic Location
- ✔ Income
- ✔ Marital Status
- ✔ Military Experience
- ✔ Parental Status
- ✔ Religious Beliefs
- ✔ Work Experience

Loden, Marilyn and Judy B. Rosener,
*Workforce America!* (Business One Irwin, 1991)

OH 1/3 — pp. 392-93

# AFFIRMATIVE ACTION, VALUING DIFFERENCES, AND MANAGING DIVERSITY COMPARED

| Affirmative Action | Valuing Differences | Managing Diversity |
|---|---|---|
| Quantitative | Qualitative | Behavioral |
| Legally driven | Ethically driven | Strategically driven |
| Remedial | Idealistic | Pragmatic |
| Assimilation model | Diversity model | Synergy model |
| Opens doors in organization | Opens attitudes, minds and culture | Opens the system |

# QUALITY AND DIVERSITY
# NOT AN EITHER-OR

Quality versus Diversity

Quality                                    Diversity

$$\longleftrightarrow$$

Quality and Diversity

Quality

Diversity

OH 1/5 — pp. 401-2

# GETTING BUY-IN
# FOR DIVERSITY:
# WHAT'S IN IT FOR STAFF

- Solicit and pay attention to the needs and priorities of all employees

- Create options and alternatives

- Focus on the benefits to individual employees

# IDEAS CENTRAL TO A DIVERSITY MIND-SET

- Recognize that diversity is not about them; it is about us

- Face the fear of change and the perceived losses

- Create a more fluid power structure

- Shed predictable habits and learn new behaviors

- Get beyond ethnocentrism

- Emphasize common experiences that unify rather than differences that divide

- Demonstrate values through actions, not words

- Remember that diversity includes everyone

# ORGANIZATIONAL IMPERATIVES FOR MANAGING DIVERSITY

- Demonstrate commitment at the highest level
- Seek involvement and commitment from the bottom up
- Teach a wide array of management techniques that work cross culturally
- Integrate diversity into the fabric of the organization
- Expect and sustain a long-term effort
- Accept the new demographic reality
- Make rapid change the constant
- Be willing to pierce the power and work through the discomfort
- Be honest
- Spread goodwill

# CULTURE = BEHAVIORAL SOFTWARE

## AWARENESS + KNOWLEDGE = CHOICES

- All human beings are programmed by cultural "software" that determines our behavior and attitudes.

- Once we recognize what our programming teaches us, we have the capacity to control our choices.

# TEN DIMENSIONS OF CULTURE

- Sense of self and space

- Communication and language

- Dress and appearance

- Food and eating habits

- Time and time consciousness

- Relationships

- Values and norms

- Beliefs and attitudes

- Mental processes and learning

- Work habits and practices

Harris and Moran *Managing Cultural Differences*, Houston, Gulf Press, 1979.

# HELPING OTHERS ACCULTURATE

- Explain the reasons

- Show the benefits

- Suggest resources

- Spend nonwork time together

- Talk about differences

# CULTURAL SOURCES OF MISUNDERSTANDING

✔ Degree of directness

✔ Appropriate subjects for conversation

✔ Facial expressions and eye contact

✔ Touch

✔ Loudness and pitch

✔ Silence

# COMMUNICATING WITH LIMITED-ENGLISH-SPEAKING STAFF

- ✔ Make it visual
- ✔ Show and tell
- ✔ Use their language
- ✔ Take it easy
- ✔ Keep it simple
- ✔ Say it again
- ✔ Assume confusion
- ✔ Get help
- ✔ Walk in their shoes
- ✔ Smile, don't laugh

# PROVIDING CONSTRUCTIVE FEEDBACK WITHOUT LOSS OF FACE

✔ Position the feedback as a benefit to the receiver

✔ Build a relationship first

✔ Go from subtle to more direct

✔ Make observations not judgments, about behaviors and conditions

✔ Use passive rather than active voice

✔ Be positive, telling what you *do* want

✔ Give feedback to group rather than individuals

✔ Make it low key

✔ Use an intermediary

✔ Assure the individual of your respect

　　　　　　　OH 3/3 — pp. 79-83

# CULTURAL NORMS AFFECTING CONFLICT IN A DIVERSE ENVIRONMENT

✔ Conflict is seen as disruptive to harmony

✔ Conflict presents a potential loss of face

✔ Culturally influenced communication style differences can make resolution of conflict more difficult

✔ There is a risk of misinterpreting conflict as being rooted in discrimination and prejudice

# TIPS FOR RESOLVING CONFLICT WITH STAFF

✔ Use the indirect approach

✔ Emphasize harmony

✔ Clarify the cultural influences operating

✔ Work with informal leaders

✔ Get specific

✔ Get honest with yourself

✔ Find out how conflicts are resolved in the other's culture

✔ Keep options open

✔ Capitalize on the relationship

✔ Respect, respect, respect

# RECOGNIZING HOW CULTURAL LENSES IMPACT TEAMSMANSHIP

✔ Desire for harmony

✔ Social status based on family or connections

✔ Emphasis on the group

✔ Fatalism and external locus of control

# SIX KEY INGREDIENTS TO HIGH PERFORMANCE ON A DIVERSE TEAM

✔ Acknowledge differences

✔ Find the common ground

✔ Identify individual interests, strengths, and preferences

✔ Clarify expectations

✔ Collectively shape group culture

✔ Create a feedback loop

OH 4/4 — pp. 149-50

# THE "NO FAIL" MEETING ESSENTIALS

- Purpose

- People

- Time frame

- Participation

# THE MEETING ENVIRONMENT

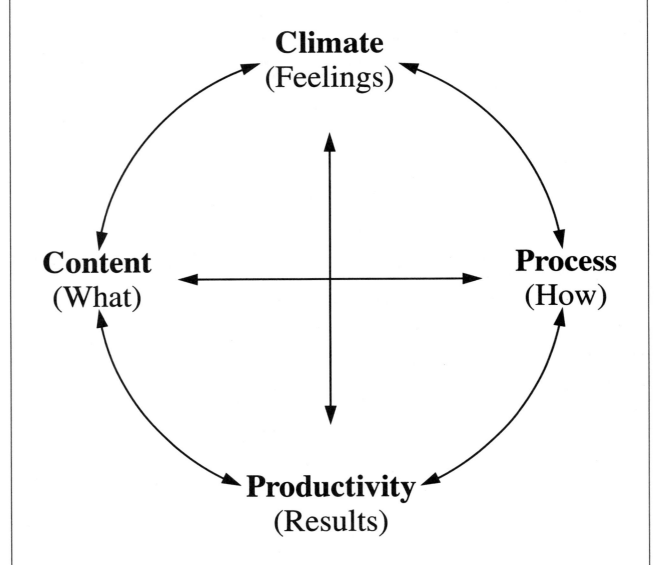

**Climate**
(Feelings)

**Content**
(What)

**Process**
(How)

**Productivity**
(Results)

# THE KINDS OF MEETINGS

- Problem solving

- Idea generating

- Decision making

- Information giving

- Data gathering

- Sharing

- Planning

- Evaluation and follow-up

# THE IMPACT OF CULTURAL NORMS ON MEETINGS

- Respect for authority

- Emphasis on group over individual

- Fear of shame and loss of face

- More contextual, less direct communication

- Value placed on harmony and collaboration

- Family as the first priority

- Time consciousness

- Problem-solving style

- Influence of fatalism on goal setting and planning

# SEVEN WAYS TO BOOST MEETING PRODUCTIVITY

- Let staff know what's expected

- Create a comfortable tone

- Use small groups and design interactive meetings

- Group people cross-culturally

- Write down the meeting's content

- Develop tools to evaluate your meetings

- Value all contributions and have patience

# SOURCES OF RESISTANCE TO PERFORMANCE EVALUATION

- Fear of repercussion

- "Not one of us" syndrome

- Lack of understanding of the process

- It is a "foreign" experience

- All task and no relationship

# DIVERSITY-RELATED INFLUENCES ON PERFORMANCE REVIEW

- Avoidance of loss of face
- Emphasis on harmony
- Respect for authority
- External locus of control
- Emphasis on relationship rather than task
- Difficulty in separating self from performance
- Emphasis on group over individual
- Lack of common base of experience
- Previous discrimination

# EMPLOYEE EVALUATION TOOLS THAT CAN ENHANCE PERFORMANCE IN ANY CULTURE

- YOU

- The employee

- Talk first, paper second

- Performance-based criteria

- Patience

# ORGANIZATIONAL BARRIERS TO DIVERSITY

✔ Cost of implementation

✔ Fear of hiring underskilled, uneducated employees

✔ Strong belief in a system that favors merit

✔ Annoyance at reverse discrimination

✔ Perception of progress

✔ Not a top-priority issue

✔ Impact on existing systems

✔ Sheer size of the organization

# LOSSES EXPERIENCED DURING CHANGE

✔ Attachments

✔ Turf

✔ Structure

✔ Future

✔ Meaning

✔ Control

William Bridges, Ph.D. *Surviving Corporate Transition*, Doubleday 1988

# NORMAL TRANSITION CURVE: HOW WE DEAL WITH CHANGE

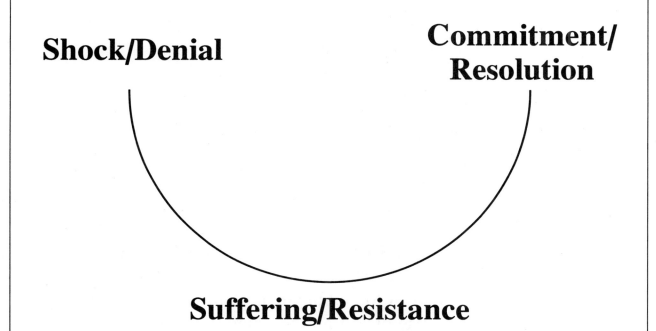

**Shock/Denial**

**Commitment/ Resolution**

**Suffering/Resistance**

Dennis T. Jaffe and Cynthia D. Scott, *Managing Organizational Change*, Los Altos, Ca, Crisp Publications, 1989.     OH 7/3 — pp. 245-49

# STAGES OF INTEGRATION

**Stage 1 Behavior:  Rejection/Resistance**
Characterized by fear of acculturation due
to sublimating one's culture. The stakes
for belonging are seen as too high.

**Stage 2 Behavior:  Isolation**
Characterized by physical and
psychological withdrawal.
There is a perfunctory politeness,
but superficial interaction.

**Stage 3 Behavior:  Assimilation**
Characterized by adjustments toward
group norms. There is a clarity about
the operating rules.

**Stage 4 Behavior:  Coexistence**
Characterized by an ability to become
part of the mainstream while maintaining
sense of self and uniqueness.

**Stage 5 Behavior:  Integration**
Characterized by a sense of belonging.
Relationships are real and fluid and
involve conflict and cooperation.

*Source:* Adapted from Eileen Morley, "Management Integration," paper presented at OD '80-A conference on Current Theory and Practice in Organizational Development, San Diego, 1980.                OH 7/4 — pp. 256-59

# THE ROLE OF ASSESSMENT: WHAT IT CAN DO

✔ Provide feedback

✔ Determine baseline data

✔ Make latent issues public

✔ Identify staff development needs

✔ Generate commitment through input

# STRUCTURING AN EFFECTIVE AUDIT

✔ What do you want to find out?

✔ What part does this data collection play in your larger organizational plan?

✔ Who needs to be involved?

✔ Where can we find the information we need?

✔ How will the data generated be used and communicated to others?

✔ What are the most useful methods and tools we can use to collect data?

✔ Who should coordinate and conduct the audit?

✔ What cultural factors may influence the audit process?

✔ What kind of budget do we have?

# ASSESSMENT METHODS

QUESTIONNAIRE

INTERVIEWS

FOCUS GROUPS

# MANAGING DIVERSITY

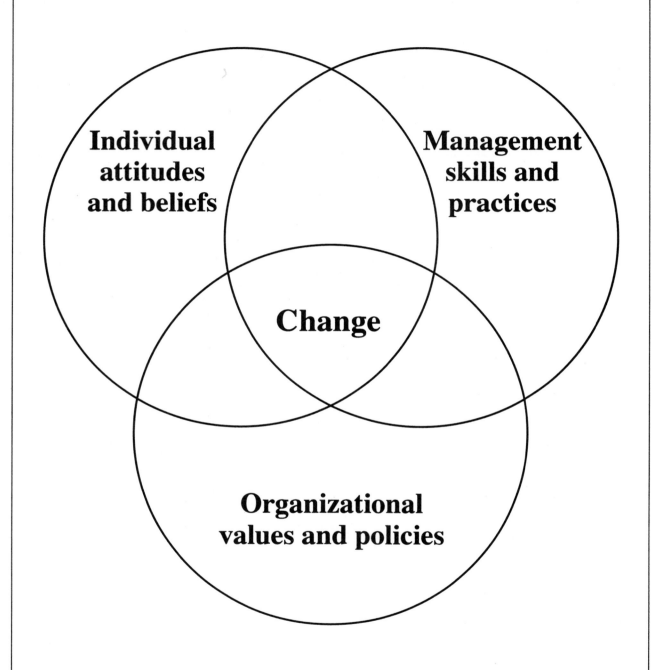

Individual attitudes and beliefs

Management skills and practices

Change

Organizational values and policies

OH 8/4 — pp. 267-71

# STAGES OF DIVERSITY

MONOCULTURAL

NONDISCRIMINATORY

MULTICULTURAL

Jackson & Holvino in "Workforce Diversity in Business,"
*Training and Development Journal*, April, 1988.

OH 8/5 — pp. 274-79

# DIVERSITY NEEDS ANALYSIS

AWARENESS

KNOWLEDGE

SKILLS

# THE IMPACT OF VALUES: DIFFERENCES IN YOUR HIRING AND PROMOTION PROCESS

| Mainstream America | Most Other Cultures |
| --- | --- |
| Work and obligation to job are high priority - - - - - - - | Primary obligation is to family and friends |
| Termination is accepted - - - - - - - - - - - - - - - - - - - - - - - - - - - | Employment is lifetime |
| Personal achievement is a strong drive - - - - - - - - - - - - - | Personal achievement is frowned upon |
| Competition - - - - - - - - - - - - - - - - - - - | Collaboration |
| Loyalty is to organization - - - - - - - - - - - | Loyalty is to individual boss or informal leader |

# TIPS FOR CREATIVE CROSS-CULTURAL NETWORKING

✔ Consciously build relationships with good people of all persuasions

✔ Broadcast available jobs

✔ Have patience in building relationships and try the indirect approach

✔ Give as well as take

✔ Acknowledge and show respect for special events of different cultures

✔ Follow up

✔ Spend time in places where you can increase your contacts

✔ Set networking goals to expand contacts

# HOW TO ASK INTERVIEW QUESTIONS IN A DIVERSE ENVIRONMENT

- Open-ended questions

- Closed-ended questions

- Speculative questions

- "Tell me ..."

- "Describe ..."

# AREAS OF INTERVIEWING ASSUMPTIONS AND BIASES

- Language skills/usage

- Communication style (verbal and nonverbal)

- Etiquette

- Social values

# UNCONSCIOUS FACTORS THAT INFLUENCE PROMOTION

➥ The clone effect

➥ Comfort level

➥ Expectations and socialization

➥ Double standard

OH 10/1 — pp. 354-56

# TRADITIONALLY PROMOTABLE QUALITIES: MALE CHARACTERISTICS

- Leading by command and control

- Exchanging rewards for services rendered

- Reliance on positional power

- Following a hierarchical, quasi-military structure

- Action orientation

- Analytical thinking and linear problem solving

Judy B. Rosener, Ph.D., "Ways Women Lead,"
*Harvard Business Review*, Nov.-Dec. 1990.                OH 10/2 — pp. 356-59

# TRADITIONALLY PROMOTABLE QUALITIES: FEMALE CHARACTERISTICS

- Sharing power and information

- Enhancing self-worth of others

- Encouraging participation

- Getting others excited about their work

Judy B. Rosener, Ph.D., "Ways Women Lead," *Harvard Business Review*, Nov.-Dec. 1990.

OH 10/3 — pp. 359-61

# CROSS-CULTURAL COACHING: WAYS TO GET TOP PERFORMANCE

- Know and appreciate different cultures

- Provide support

- Give helpful and usable feedback

- Teach the importance of cause and effect

- Point out the big (or whole) picture

- Teach promotable skills

- Create a collaborative partnership

# CAREER DEVELOPMENT MODEL

TOP DOWN

- Performance Review

- Recruitment/Hiring/Promotion

- Accountability

- Training

# CAREER DEVELOPMENT MODEL

## BOTTOM UP

| Managers | Employees |
| --- | --- |
| Give performance reviews sensitively | Build connections |
| Handle intercultural conflict | Become politically savvy |
| Run meetings effectively | Position ideas effectively |
| Conduct interviews in culturally appropriate ways | Manage change |
| Build effective multicultural work teams | Become assertive |
| Recognize own biases in promotions | Gain self-promotion skills |
| Value a wider range of management behaviors | |

# Bibliography

Bridges, William. *Surviving Corporate Transition*. New York: Doubleday, 1988.

Harris, Philip R., and Robert T. Moran. *Managing Cultural Differences*. Houston: Gulf, 1979, pp. 190–95.

Morley, Eileen. "Management Integration." Paper presented at OD '80—A Conference on Current Theory and Practice in Organizational Development, San Diego, March 1980.

The Hudson Report. *Workforce 2000*. Towers Perren & Hudson Institute.

Foster, Badi G.; Gerald Jackson; William Cross; and Rita Hardeman. "Workforce Diversity and Business." *Training and Development Journal*, April 1988, pp. 38–42.

Jaffe, Dennis T., and Cynthia D. Scott. *Managing Organizational Change*. Los Altos, Calif.: Crisp Publications, 1989.

Loden, Marilyn, and Judy B. Rosener. *Workforce America! Managing Employee Diversity as a Vital Resource*. Burr Ridge, Ill.: Irwin Professional Publishing, 1991.

Rosener, Judy B. "Ways Women Lead." *Harvard Business Review*, November/December 1990, pp. 119–25.